The Prison-House of Language

We have to cease to think if we
refuse to do it in the prison-house of language;
for we cannot reach further than the
doubt which asks whether the limit we see
is really a limit. . .

NIETZSCHE

The Prison-House of Language

A Critical Account of Structuralism
and Russian Formalism

By Fredric Jameson

Princeton University Press, Princeton, N.J.

Preface

THE HISTORY OF thought is the history of its models. Classical mechanics, the organism, natural selection, the atomic nucleus or electronic field, the computer: such are some of the objects or systems which, first used to organize our understanding of the natural world, have then been called upon to illuminate human reality.

The lifetime of any given model knows a fairly predictable rhythm. Initially, the new concept releases quantities of new energies, permits hosts of new perceptions and discoveries, causes a whole dimension of new problems to come into view, which result in turn in a volume of new work and research. Throughout this initial stage the model itself remains stable, for the most part serving as a medium through which a new view of the universe may be obtained and catalogued.

In the declining years of the model's history, a proportionately greater amount of time has to be spent in readjusting the model itself, in bringing it back into line with its object of study. Now research tends to become theoretical rather than practical, and to turn back upon its own presuppositions (the structure of the model itself), finding itself vexed by the false problems and dilemmas into which the inadequacy of the model seems increasingly to lead it. One thinks, for example, of the ether or of collective consciousness.

At length the model is exchanged for a new one. This momentous event has been described by some of the thinkers with whom this book is concerned as a kind of *mutation* (itself an excellent example of the metaphoric application of one model to a wholly different field of study). It is certain, indeed, that such a replacement marks an absolute break, an absolute end and the beginning of something hitherto unprecedented, even if it cannot always be dated as cleanly as a single revolutionary experiment or the publication of a single decisive work. Nor, it would seem, can the new be consciously prepared, any more than those dissatisfied with the old paradigm can, by taking thought, simply devise some new one out of whole cloth.

Such was indeed the history of the organic model, that concept of the organism as a prototype which with a single spark touched off Romantic philosophy and nineteenth century scientific thinking. The advantage of the notion of organism was that in it the realms of the diachronic and the synchronic found a living synthesis, or rather had not yet been separated, for it is the diachronic (the observation of gradual changes in the organism) which leads the attention of the observer to the synchronic structure (those organs which have changed and evolved and which are now to be understood in their simultaneous coexistence with each other in the life of the organism itself). Such notions as *function* are thus to be found at the very intersection between the two dimensions, and with them history wins its claim to be an independent mode of understanding in its own right.

Yet in the long run the organic model relies too heavily on substantialist thinking. If its objects of study are not given in advance as autonomous entities, it tends to invent fictive ones for methodological purposes, as in the various organic theories of society or culture. Of the reactions against such substantialist thinking, of the various images of "field" or of relationality, none has been more thoroughgoing than that which now proposes as its basic model language itself.

Language as a model! To rethink everything through once again in terms of linguistics! What is surprising, it would seem, is only that no one ever thought of doing so before; for of all the elements of consciousness and of social life, language would appear to enjoy some incomparable onto-logical priority, of a type yet to be determined. It will be objected that to describe the Structuralist enterprise this way is to admit that it recapitulates the earlier problematics of the history of philosophy, that it returns to pre-Marxist and indeed pre-Hegelian conceptual dilemmas and false problems with which we no longer have to concern our-selves. Yet this holds true, as we shall see later in the present essay, more for the ultimate contradictions of Structuralism than for its concrete daily work: the latter, its content—the organization and status of Language—furnishes a new body of material in terms of which the old problems are raised again in new and unforeseen ways. Thus to "refuse" Structuralism on ideological grounds amounts to declin-ing the task of integrating present-day linguistic discov-eries into our philosophical systems; my own feeling is that a genuine critique of Structuralism commits us to working our way completely through it so as to emerge, on the other side, into some wholly different and theoretically more satisfying philosophical perspective.

This is not to say that the very point of departure of Structuralism—the primacy of the linguistic model—is wholly unrelated to the conceptual dilemmas with which we shall shortly be concerned: for such a starting point is no less arbitrary for being unique, and the systems of thought which emerge from it will not themselves be exempt from some eventual, problematical, and painful reexamination of their own enabling premise.

One is tempted to evoke the antinomies of pre-Socratic thought, which sought to isolate the single constitutive element of the world's fabric—let us say water or fire—only to find that the constitution of water or fire itself would have to be of a different type. To be sure, when today we say that everything is ultimately historical, or economic, or sexual, or indeed *linguistic*, we mean thereby not so much that phenomena are made up, in their very bone and blood cells, by such raw material, but rather that they are susceptible to analysis by those respective methods.

Yet there result analogous paradoxes. Nothing could be more fitting, one would think, than the application of linguistic methods to literature, itself essentially a linguistic structure. Yet the older stylistics, that of Spitzer and Auerbach, or more recently of J.-P. Richard, worked much more closely with the verbal texture of the work itself. We find ourselves ultimately before the conclusion that the attempt to see the literary work as a linguistic system is in reality the application of a *metaphor*.

Such dialectical reversals may also be found at the outer limits of the system. I think, for example, of Greimas' description of the object of study of a structural semantics as a *meaning-effect*: as though, having taken all meanings for our object, we can no longer speak about them in terms of signification as such, and find ourselves obliged somehow to take a position outside the realm of meanings in order to judge what they all, irrespective of their content, have formally in common with each other. Expression as a content turns out to demand impression as its form, and we end up having to describe a structure of intellection in terms of what it "feels like" to think it.

The deeper justification for the use of the linguistic model or metaphor must, I think, be sought elsewhere, outside the claims and counterclaims for scientific validity or technological progress. It lies in the concrete character of the social life of the so-called advanced countries today, which offer the spectacle of a world from which nature as such has been eliminated, a world saturated with messages and information, whose intricate commodity network may be seen as the very prototype of a system of signs. There is therefore a profound consonance between linguistics as a method and that systematized and disembodied nightmare which is our culture today.

The present survey does not aim at a sociological analysis of the new linguistic disciplines. It does not even pretend to offer a historical and anecdotal account of the developments of the movements in question. Such an account, for the Formalists, is available to the English-speaking reader in Victor Erlich's definitive *Russian Formalism* (The Hague, 1955), which traces the destiny of Formalism from its origins in meetings of linguists and literary students in Petersburg and Moscow during the First World War to its disappearance as a recognizable polemic posture in the fateful year 1929.

Nothing comparable exists for Structuralism, whose rise as a "mass movement" may be conveniently dated from the publication of Lévi-Strauss' *Tristes tropiques* in 1955, and which may be said to have reached a zenith of sorts (following such important sign-posts as the foundation of *Tel Quel* in 1960 and the publication of Lévi-Strauss' *La Pensée sauvage* in 1962) with the twin appearance, during the 1966-1967 season, of Lacan's already legendary *Écrits* and of Derrida's three major texts. As far as the term "Structuralism" is concerned, I understand it in the strictest and most limited sense of work based on the metaphor or model of a linguistic system: it would thus not apply to Jean Piaget or Lucien Goldmann, both of whom have appropriated it for their own systems; nor would it bear any relationship to the usage of certain schools of American sociology. I should, however, add that I have deliberately excluded from the present work any treatment of the very rich materials of Soviet Structuralism, as developed by Yury M. Lotman and his colleagues at the University of Tartu.

My own plan—to offer an introductory survey of these movements which might stand at the same time as a critique of their ·basic methodology—is no doubt open to attack from both partisans and adversaries alike (partisans and adversaries of Structuralism, that is, for does Formalism still have adversaries? does it still have partisans?). The present critique does not, however, aim at judgments of detail, nor at the expression of some opinion, either positive or negative, on the works in question here. It proposes rather to lay bare what Collingwood would have called the "absolute presuppositions" of Formalism and Structuralism taken as intellectual totalities. These absolute presuppositions may then speak for themselves, and, like all such ultimate premises or models, are too fundamental to be either accepted or rejected.

Nor will my findings, bearing essentially on the perspectives and distortions produced by synchronic thinking, come as any surprise, although the consequences of the synchronic system have not, I believe, been worked out elsewhere in such detail as this.

I am tempted to qualify my critique at the very outset and to make my own that distinction between real history and diachronic thinking which has been, as the reader will see later, insisted on by some Structuralists. My guiding thread and permanent preoccupation in these pages has been to clarify the relationships possible between the synchronic methods of Saussurean linguistics and the realities of time and history itself. Nowhere has such a relationship proved more paradoxical than in that realm of literary analysis in which the most tangible and lasting achievements of Formalism and Structuralism have been made. I refer to the analysis of narrative structures, from Shklovsky and Propp to Lévi-Strauss and Greimas. The paradox is, of course, that a synchronic method should yield so rich and suggestive a view of the very forms through which the mind sees change and events in time.

What if one could go even further than this? In their years of reason the Formalists (and it was due not only to the pressure of Stalinism) developed into literary historians of what one hesitates to call the traditional variety, when they did not seek their fortune elsewhere, in the historical novel and in the movies. The Formalists' image of literary history as mutation is, as the reader will discover, both philosophically unsatisfactory and imaginatively stimulating.

As for Structuralism, who could claim that a thinker like Lévi-Strauss—thanks to whom all the apparently outmoded reflections of Rousseau on the state of nature and the social contract have once more become the order of the day; thanks to whom, in the midst of a stifling and artificial civilization, the meditation on the very origins of culture has been reawakened—has not made an impact on our thinking about history? And we will suggest in the following pages that if Structuralism has any ultimate and privileged field of study, it may well be found in the history of ideas conceived of in a new and rigorous fashion.

To say, in short, that synchronic systems cannot deal in any adequate conceptual way with temporal phenomena is not to say that we do not emerge from them with a heightened sense of the mystery of diachrony itself. We have tended to take temporality for granted; where everything is historical, the idea of history itself has seemed to empty of content. Perhaps that is, indeed, the ultimate propaedeutic value of the linguistic model: to renew our fascination with the seeds of time.

La Jolla
March, 1972

Contents

I

The Linguistic Model

MEANING or language? Logic or linguistics? Such are the fateful alternatives which account for the immense disparity between British and continental philosophy today, between the analytical or common language school and what has become, almost before our very eyes, Structuralism. Origins are as emblematic as the results themselves, and it is therefore fitting, for a moment at the outset, to juxtapose the *Cours de linguistique générale* of Ferdinand de Saussure, published in 1916, three years after his death, from a set of collated lecture notes, with such a characteristic product of the Anglo-American tradition as C. K. Ogden and I. A. Richards' *The Meaning of Meaning*, which first appeared in 1922.

These two works, each immensely influential, have something revealing and symptomatic to tell us about the cultural areas to which their respective influence has been limited. It would be tempting, but not quite accurate, to see in them two mutually exclusive modes of thought, to hold them up as the antithesis between the analytical and the dialectical understanding. It may be more adequate to account for the divergence through some initial ambiguity in their object of study, through the unique structure of language itself, with its twin faces, of which Saussure has said, in a famous image, that it is "comparable to a sheet of paper: thought being the recto and sound the verso; one cannot cut one side without at the same time cutting the other; and in the same way, in language, one can neither isolate sound from thought nor thought from sound."[1]

[1] Ferdinand de Saussure, *Cours de linguistique générale* (Paris, 1965, third edition), p. 157.

Yet each side is the starting point, not even for a different philosophy, but for a wholly different discipline itself. If we have in this book to deal with the return of linguistics as a model and an informing metaphor to that literary and philosophical realm from which, as a science, it once declared its independence, then it is just as certain that it returns with all the prestige of science itself; while, with symbolic logic, its philosophical alternative also conquers its methodological autonomy upon the ruins of systematic philosophizing after the death of Hegel.

The Anglo-American approach has of course its philosophical and ideological roots in the long tradition of British empiricism, which in some ways it prolongs. In the same way, it is difficult to assess the originality of Saussure without forming some preliminary idea of the state of linguistics when he came to it, in order to be in a position to appreciate what it was he came to change.

As in the other disciplines, so also in linguistics the Romantic movement, the primacy of the middle classes, was the signal for a thoroughgoing reevaluation of all outstanding problems, as well as solutions, in new and historical terms. In linguistics, the preference of classical thought for eternal, changeless, normative laws had resulted in that close identification of language with logic whose codification we know as grammar. The Romantic age replaced grammar with philology; and it was characterized by a sudden proliferation of great historical discoveries (Grimm's law, Bopp's reconstruction of Indo-European, the elaboration of the great schools of Romance and Germanic philology, particularly by German scholars) and the ultimate codification of these discoveries as laws of language by the Neo-Grammarians, and particularly by Hermann Paul, whose ideas may stand as the dominant intellectual current

4

in linguistics during the period when Saussure undertook his first studies.

1

We may assume that the elaboration of dogma coincides with the exhaustion of the vein. In any case, Saussure's innovations may be understood first and foremost as a reaction against the doctrines of the Neo-Grammarians. For the interest in change and evolution, in the reconstruction of proto-languages and the determination of language families and their inner affiliations, had led in the long run to Paul's conviction that "what is not historical in linguistics is not scientific."[2] Against this, Saussure's separation of the synchronic from the diachronic, of historical from structural research, is equally absolute, and contains a methodological presupposition which is just as peremptory a value judgment: "to the degree that something is meaningful, it will be found to be synchronic."[3]

But Saussure's starting point is more than a mere reaction; it is at the same time a liberation of intellectual energies. For with this distinction between diachrony and synchrony (he seems to have invented the terms in this form, although they were known before him in other acceptations in geology), he is able to demonstrate the existence of two mutually exclusive forms of understanding as well. Historical philology, in this light, proves to have taken as its object only individual changes, isolated facts; even its laws are somehow local and contingent: they are, we may say, scientific but meaningless. Saussure's originality was to have insisted on the fact that language as a total system is complete

[2] Quoted by Milka Ivić, *Trends in Linguistics* (The Hague, 1965), p. 61.
[3] Quoted in É. Buyssens, "La Linguistique synchronique de Saussure" (*Cahiers Ferdinand de Saussure*, Vol. xviii [1961], pp. 17-33).

at every moment, no matter what happens to have been altered in it a moment before. This is to say that the temporal model proposed by Saussure is that of a series of complete systems succeeding each other in time; that language is for him a perpetual present, with all the possibilities of meaning implicit in its every moment.

Saussure's *is* in a sense an existential perception: no one denies the *fact* of the diachronic, that sounds have their own history and that meanings change. Only for the speaker, at any moment in the history of the language, one meaning alone exists, the current one: words have no memory. This view of language is confirmed rather than refuted by the appeal to etymology, as Jean Paulhan has shown in an ingenious little book. For etymology, as it is used in daily life, is to be considered not so much a scientific fact as a rhetorical form, the illicit use of historical causality to support the drawing of logical consequences ("the word itself tells us so: *etymology, etumos logos*, authentic meaning. Thus etymology advertises itself, and sends us back to itself as its own first principle"[4]).

We may express all this in yet another way by showing that the ontological foundations of the synchronic and the diachronic are quite different from each other. The former lies in the immediate lived experience of the native speaker; the latter rests on a kind of intellectual construction, the result of comparisons between one moment of lived time and another by someone who stands outside, who has thus substituted a purely intellectual continuity for a lived one. In short, we may ask what it means to say that, for instance, "etymology" and *etumos logos* are the same. The same for whom? On what principle is this identity, which crosses generations of individual lives and the extinction of untold numbers of concrete pronunciations, founded? If the ques-

[4] Jean Paulhan, *La Preuve par l'étymologie* (Paris, 1953), p. 12.

tion seems unduly ingenious, that is because we are still caught up in all kinds of positivistic presuppositions, because the position of the observer is still being taken for granted and has not yet come to strike us as problematical.

The first principle of Saussure's work is therefore an anti-historical one, and we will understand its meaning better if we see just what role its discovery played in his life. Saussure seems to have been a reluctant revolutionary: his innovations are not the work of someone instinctively out of step with his own time, of someone from the very beginning restless and dissatisfied with the modes of thought he found dominant as a young man, but rather of someone who was his whole life long involved in the teaching and propagation of precisely those diachronic, Neo-Grammarian doctrines against which his posthumous work stood as an attack. His major publication in his own lifetime, the *Mémoire sur le système primitif des voyelles dans les langues indoeuropéennes*, the work by which his contemporaries knew him and which he had published in 1879 at the age of twenty-two, was one of the crowning achievements of the Neo-Grammarian school, a deduction on diachronic principles the effect of which was to demonstrate the hidden regularity of certain sound patterns which had hitherto been taken as "exceptions" to the "laws" already codified. It is therefore permitted to conjecture that he arrived at the key notion of the separation between synchrony and diachrony—or, to put it in more positive terms, he developed the concept of a *system*—out of increasing dissatisfaction with his experience of history itself, and with the kinds of thinking and explanation he found possible there, a dissatisfaction based not so much on the absence of general laws as on their very abundance, on their secret hollowness for the mind. In short, one can well understand how in the face of all the tables of sound changes Saussure found himself

7

little by little evolving a distinction between causes that are external to a phenomenon and causes which are somehow intrinsic to it, and this distinction may stand as the definition of the idea of system itself. What is at stake is the whole notion of law itself, as a meaningful explanation satisfying to the mind. To be sure, the patterns of diachronic changes are regular and can be formulated in predictable recurrent patterns; Saussure did so himself in the striking example mentioned above. But this merely empirical fact of regularity has no meaning in the linguistic system because it derives from causes—geographical barriers, migration and population shifts—outside the language itself. The law thus represents, we may say, a leap from the terms of one series (language patterns) to the terms of another (geographical law or population movements).

diachronic →

We may illustrate this disparity perhaps more clearly in an illustration drawn from history itself. I am thinking, for instance, of Pieter Geyl's revision of the classic interpretation of the religious and cultural split between the Protestant Netherlands and Catholic Belgium.[5] What is in question is no doubt the inevitability of the boundary line; yet in historical matters, as is well known, we may take the word "inevitable" as the sign, not of any deterministic presuppositions, but simply of the sheer comprehensibility of a given event in the terms of the historical understanding itself. For the earlier historians, this split was somehow an "inevitable" one, for it reflected a basic cultural difference between the populations on either side. To the north, the Protestant population resisted the Spaniards for religious reasons; to the south, the Catholic rebels against the crown were less intransigent and easier to subdue. Later on, with Pirenne

[5] See Pieter Geyl, "The National State and the Writers of Netherlands History," in *Debates with Historians* (London, 1955), pp. 179-197.

8

and his school, we come to another version of this same
thesis, the terms of whose translation, however, reflect pro-
French sympathies rather than the Protestant ones clearly
in evidence in the earlier formulation. Pirenne's doctrine of
a genuine autonomous cultural tradition in Flanders that
extended back into the middle ages results in the same general conclusion, namely that the ultimate national boundary
was little more than a ratification of a profound and already
existing division between the two areas.

Geyl has little difficulty showing the immediate political
and polemic ends served by these various theses at those
conjunctures in Dutch or Belgian history when they were
proposed; his own solution is, as one might suspect, a re-
ductive, debunking one. He is able to dismiss the earlier
theories by pointing out what everyone had known all
along, that there was no greater concentration of Protestant-
ism in the north than in the south, and by showing that
the present-day religious and national frontier falls together
with a geographical one, namely with the beginning of the
area of the great rivers in the north in which the Protestant
armies entrenched themselves, and into which Parma's army
was not strong enough to penetrate. Given this ceasefire line
conditioned by natural obstacles, cultural pacification pro-
ceeded briskly on either side and the relative religious
homogeneity of present-day Belgium or Holland is not really
a matter for much astonishment.

I have introduced this illustration, not to make any comment on the historical thesis presented in it, but rather to
underline the various effects on the mind of different types
of historical explanations. Geyl's theory is, I would like to
say, diachronically satisfying as the history of history: insofar as it is itself the resolution of a historical riddle, prepared by the presentation and successive rejection of the
earlier historical positions, it has great elegance for the mind.

pre or un Hegelian

But in itself, synchronically, there is something more disturbing about it: its thrust is to place the ultimate source of the comprehensibility of history outside human action itself, in the contingent accidents of the non-human environment; to locate the ultimate term of the chain of cause-and-effect outside history, in geology, in the brute physical fact of the disposition of the geographical terrain. This final term has of course its own history (the origin of the great rivers at an earlier moment in the earth's development, the formation of the deltas, the chemical composition of the soil deposited there), but *that* history is a series which has nothing in common with the series of purely human events, a different series entirely, on a vaster and indeed incommensurate scale. I am even tempted to say that the very notion of the type of series itself, the distinction between internal and external causes, which may strike the reader as an unanalyzed presupposition smuggled into the discussion, is in reality implicit in Geyl's theory itself: for the force of his trick ending depends precisely on a shift from human to inhuman forms of causation.

I am, of course, not suggesting a return to the kind of idealistic history which Geyl's theory is concerned here to refute, and which foresees a holding together, within a common conceptual framework, of such incommensurate realities as human action and geological upheaval. It is, however, worth pointing out that the fact of the great rivers can never have been felt as contingent by the neighboring populations, and must already have been integrated, as a form of meaning, into their respective cultures long before its return upon them, with renewed contingency, in the form of the external influence under discussion here. The very notion of contingency or "hasard" reminds us that the Saussurean revolution is contemporaneous with theories of "pure poetry" and with the struggle, within the aesthetic realm as well, to eliminate the last

10

traces of the extrinsic or the contingent from poetic lan- ⎫
guage itself. We may best dramatize the value of Saussure's
linguistic solution by pointing out that even for historiog-
raphy there is yet another solution conceivable, alongside
that of Geyl or of the meta-history which he attacks: this
would be a type of structural history in which the relationship between Holland and Flanders would be studied
within the context of a certain number of oppositions
(Catholic-Protestant, Flemish-Walloon), which may then
be combined or coordinated in a series of permutations or
determinate relationships. From such a point of view the
earlier combinations would be as little relevant as the
previous casts of dice in a given succession.

In any case, it was some analogous feeling for the radical
incompatibility of the various explanation systems which
must have been at work in Saussure's mind during the
elaboration of his own theories. This is still, of course, a
negative way of putting it; and in this sense Saussure's
thought is but one among many contemporary reactions
against positivism. It is precisely his notion of a system
which distinguishes him from the idealistic and humanistic,
anti-scientific revolt which we find in the late-nineteenth-
century religious revival and in Bergson and Croce and
the linguistic movements which developed out of them.
Saussure's position has many affinities with that of Husserl,
for like Husserl he was not content simply to point out the
existence of another equally valuable mode of humanistic
and qualitative thought alongside the scientific and quanti-
tative, but tried to codify the structure of such thought ⎞
in a methodological way, thus making all kinds of new and ⎠
concrete investigations possible.

Saussure's dissatisfaction with the older linguistics was
in its very essence a methodological, a terminological one.
When one reflects on the relative obscurity of Saussure

11

during his own lifetime, when one examines the slight volume of his published work and learns something of the posthumous history of his manuscripts, it is difficult to escape the feeling that there is something archetypal about Saussure's silence. It is that same legendary and august renunciation of speech of which the gesture of Rimbaud is emblematic, but which recurs again and again in the early modern period in different guises and different forms, in the reticence of Wittgenstein, in Valéry's long abandonment of poetry for mathematics, in the testament of Kafka and in Hofmannsthal's "Letter from Lord Chandos." All of them testify to a kind of geological shift in language itself, to the gradual deterioration in this transition period to new thought patterns, of the inherited terminology and even the inherited grammar and syntax. "Wovon man nicht sprechen kann, darüber muss man schweigen." Yet the famous sentence, in that it can be spoken at all, carries its own paradox within itself. So it is that we learn what we know of these silences, not through the official art forms which have been emptied of their meaning, but through secondary and impermanent media, through reminiscences and snatches of conversation, through letters and fragments. It is, in fact, in a letter to Antoine Meillet that Saussure's peculiar anxiety is preserved for us:

"But I'm sick of it all and of the general difficulty of writing any ten lines of a common sense nature in connection with linguistic facts. Having so long busied myself with the logical classification of such facts and with the classification of the points of view from which we examine them, I begin to be more and more aware of the immense labor that would be necessary to show the linguist *what he is really up to* when he reduces each operation to the appropriate category; and at the same time to show the not inconsiderable vanity of everything one ends up being able to do in linguistics.

"In the last analysis, only the picturesque side of a language still holds my interest, what makes it different from all the others insofar as it belongs to a particular people with a particular origin, the almost ethnographic side of language: and precisely I can no longer give myself over without reserve to that kind of study, to the appreciation of a particular fact from a particular milieu.

"The utter ineptness of current terminology, the need for reform, and to show what kind of an object language is in general—these things over and over again spoil whatever pleasure I can take in historical studies, even though I have no greater wish than not to have to bother myself with these general linguistic considerations.

"Much against my own inclination all this will end up with a book in which I will explain without any passion or enthusiasm how there is not a single term used in linguistics today which has any meaning for me whatsoever. And only after that, I'm afraid, will I be able to take up my work again where I left it."[6]

The transition witnessed by Saussure, and dramatized by the other great moments of verbal impairment alluded to above, may be described as a movement from a substantive way of thinking to a relational one, a transition nowhere quite so acute as in linguistics. The discovery of Saussure was that the cause of terminological difficulties in linguistics resulted from the fact that these terms tried to *name* substances or objects (the "word," the "sentence") while linguistics was a science characterized by the absence of such substances: "Elsewhere we find things, objects, given

[6] Letter to Antoine Meillet, 4 January 1894, *Cahiers Ferdinand de Saussure*, Vol. xxi (1964), p. 93.

13

in advance, which you are free to consider from various points of view. Here there are first of all points of view, they may be true or false but there are nothing but points of view in the beginning, with whose help you then subsequently *create* your objects. These creations turn out to correspond to realities when your point of view is correct, or not to correspond as the case may be; but in either case nothing, no object, is given at any time as existing in itself. Not even when you're looking at the most material kind of fact, one most obviously having the appearance of definition in and by itself, as would be the case with a series of vocal sounds."[7]

Thus it is on account of the peculiar nature of language as an object of study that Saussure is led to strike out in a new direction. Once again, of course, the dilemma of linguistics is only part of a vaster crisis in the sciences in general: in physics for instance, where the alternation between the wave and particle theories of light begins to cast some doubt on the conception of the atom as a substance, and where indeed the idea of a "field" is not without analogies to Saussure's notion of a system. In all these areas, scientific investigation has reached the limits of perception; its objects are no longer things or organisms which are isolated by their own physical structures from each other, and which can be dissected and classified in various ways. Saussure's concept of the "system" implies that in this new trackless unphysical reality content is form; that you can see only as much as your model permits you to see; that the methodological starting point does more than simply reveal, it actually creates, the object of study.

In personal or psychological terms, this methodological perception is reflected in existentialism, whose leitmotiv— the priority of existence over essence—is indeed simply an-

7 Quoted in Émile Benveniste, *Problèmes de linguistique générale* (Paris, 1966), p. 39.

other way of saying the same thing, and of showing how lived reality alters in function of the "choice" we make of *through* it or the essences through which we interpret it: in other *the model we interpret* words, in function of the "model" through which we see and live the world. On a larger scale, it is clear that this kind of thinking has the gravest implications for the human studies, for disciplines such as history and sociology whose object of study is almost as fluid and ill-definable as language itself. Saussure was of course well aware of this: "When a science has no immediate recognizable concrete units, then it follows that such units are not really essential to it. In history, for instance, what is the basic unit? The individual, the period, the nation? No one is sure, but what difference does it make? Historical investigations may be pursued without a final decision on this point."[8]

Thus, for units, entities, substances, are substituted values and relationships: "All of which simply means that *in language there are only differences*. More than that: a difference normally presupposes some positive terms between which it is established; but in language there are only differences *without positive terms*."[9] Saussure is here conceiving value in terms of an economic metaphor, where a given unit of currency has the same function whether it be gold or silver coin, *assignat* or wooden nickel: in other words, where the positive nature of the substance used is not as important as its function in the system.

In one sense, this distinction between value and substance has something of the force of the mind/body opposition, of the antithesis between mind and matter. One of its advantages for Saussurean linguistics is to make possible a methodological separation of pure sounds (as, for example, the articulations made by a speaker of a language utterly un-

[8] *Cours de linguistique générale*, p. 149.
[9] *Ibid.*, p. 166.

15

known to us) from meaningful sounds, or what Saussure calls acoustic images, the kinds of patterns a language begins to fall into even when we do not yet know it terribly well: that which permits us to recognize and perhaps visually to identify or to spell a foreign word even though we do not yet know its meaning. The distinction had already been anticipated by the two Polish linguists, Kruszewski and Baudouin de Courtenay (the latter later to become the teacher of the Petersburg Formalists)[10] when they foresaw the need for two wholly different kinds of science, the one an investigation of sounds in their pure physicality (phonetics), the other based on an exploration of meaning patterns ("phonologie" or phonemics). We will see the results of such a distinction later on; suffice it to say that we here witness the return of the antithesis between diachronic and synchronic on a new level, for phonetics will deal chiefly with diachronic changes, while to phonemics will fall the task of exploring the synchronic system.

Thus, philosophically, we are faced with a rather peculiar identification between change and matter, on the one hand, and meaning and the a-temporal, on the other. It should be noted that the most adequate philosophic analogies are not with the older and rather simplistic versions of the mind/body problem, but, once again, with the newer phenomenological ones, where matter becomes Husserl's *hylé*, and whose most illustrious ontological expression is found in the Sartrean antithesis between the en-soi and the pour-soi, between facticity and transcendence.

Yet the basic problem of the idea of system remains even after we make abstraction of the purely material substratum: if substances no longer exist in the ordinary sense, then

10 See Ivić, *Trends in Linguistics*, pp. 97-100.

how can relationships function, of what and in what does value consist? The point is that for Saussure the ultimate atomic units, the basic components of the system, are somehow self-defining: inasmuch as they are themselves, whatever they may turn out to be, the basic units of meaning, it is logically impossible to go beyond them and to work up some more abstract definition in terms of which they would function as members of a class. This is what Saussure expresses in a striking phrase: "The characteristics of the unit are at one with the unit itself. In language as in any semiological system, what distinguishes a sign is what constitutes it. Difference creates the characteristic (or the feature) in the same way that it creates value and the unit itself."[11] Ogden and Richards are very clear on this point when they complain, "The disadvantage of this account is . . . that the process of interpretation is included by definition in the sign!"[12]

What is meant by all this in a practical way is simply that where in a given language *ng* may be a distinctive feature, in another it will have no functional value whatsoever even if it does happen to occur, so that in this sense no generalizations are possible about the individual components of the linguistic process. Context is everything, and it is the feeling of the native speaker which remains in the last resort the test of the presence or absence of distinctive features.

In another sense, of course, we continue to discuss these phenomena in abstract and general terms: the proof, if any were needed, lies in the very project of a "general linguistics" itself. What has happened is that the mode of abstracting has shifted. Where, in earlier, substantialist

[11] *Cours de linguistique générale*, p. 168.
[12] C. K. Ogden and I. A. Richards, *The Meaning of Meaning* (London, 1960), p. 5, n. 2.

thought, abstractions were basically names for the substances (i.e., the "noun"), the new abstractions aim precisely at the meaning process itself, describe the way the
mind distinguishes signs, are resumed in the two words
"identity" and "difference," which clearly reflect a wholly
different conceptual level than the old grammatical categories. (It is worth noting that where relatively substantial
categories do survive in Saussure, as in a word like "phoneme," at that point all kinds of polemics and false problems tend to arise.)

All this—the concept of system, the notion of language
as a perception of identities and differences—is thus implicit in the initial distinction between synchrony and diachrony. It is therefore no real service to Saussure's thought
to attempt to compromise, as many of his followers have
done, by trying to show that this initial distinction is not
really so marked, not really so absolute, as its terms might
at first glance imply. The plain fact of the matter is that
one cannot have it both ways. It was precisely the unre-
lieved starkness and intransigeance of the initial antithesis
that proved the most suggestive for future development, and
on which the subsequent parts of the doctrine are founded.
Once you have begun by separating diachronic from synchronic, in other words, you can never really put them
back together again. If the opposition in the long run proves
to be a false or misleading one, then the only way to suppress it is by throwing the entire discussion onto a higher
dialectical plane, choosing a new starting point, utterly
recasting the problems involved in new terms.

It would be wrong, however, to conclude that no diachronic development whatsoever is possible in the Saussurean model, and it is instructive in this light to examine
the solution which Roman Jakobson has given to this dilem-

ma in his "Principes de phonologie historique."[13] He there points out how a diachronic change—i.e., the loss of a certain sound—results in an imbalance in the synchronic system which must then be modified to adapt to the new state of things. Where before, let us say, the available entities *a, b, c, d* combined with each other in various combinations, now all those combinations must be redistributed among the remaining *a, b, d*. This model of successive, modified synchronic systems served as the basis for Jost Trier's lexicological studies, the most famous illustration of which is the thirteenth-century Middle High German displacement of the opposition *Kunst/List* (both of them subsumed under the general category *Wisheit*) by the idea of *Wizzen*, which replaces *List* but is no longer part of *Wisheit*, so that there now remain three terms in presence of each other rather than the earlier binary antithesis, and the dyad becomes a triad.[14]

[13] Reprinted in N. S. Troubetskoy, *Principes de phonologie* (Paris, 1964).

[14] See Ivić, *Trends in Linguistics*, pp. 196-197 and Maurice Leroy, *Les Grands courants de la linguistique moderne* (Paris, 1966), pp. 166-167. Since the classic introductory essay to this work is unavailable in translation, I append some extracts. The opening paragraph, on his method: "No spoken word is as isolated in the consciousness of its speaker and listener as its phonetic isolation might lead one to conclude. Every word we pronounce carries its own conceptual opposite within it. More than that. Of the totality of conceptual relationships which throng forward at the pronunciation of a given word, that of the contrary or conceptual opposite is only one, and not even the most important. Beside it, above it, a host of other words arise which are conceptually more or less closely related to the one which has been spoken. These are its conceptual family. They constitute among themselves and with the word just spoken an articulated whole, a structure which we may call a word-field or a field of linguistic signs. . . ." (p. 1)

And the following, on the problems of diachrony: "Such a method does not constitute a denial of history and development. It would be wrong to give Being the priority over Becoming simply in reaction

19

Yet as rich and fascinating as such models of historical change may be, they are still not altogether satisfying conceptually. "If a rupture of the system's equilibrium precedes a given mutation," Jakobson tells us, "and if there results from this mutation a suppression of the disequilibrium, then we have no difficulty discovering the mutation's function: its task is *to reestablish the equilibrium.* However, when a mutation reestablishes the equilibrium at one point in the system, it may break it at other points and provoke the need for a new mutation. Thus a whole series of stabilizing mutations are produced. . . ."[15] The trouble is that the word "mutation" is being used in two different ways, or, if you prefer, that there are not one, but two mutations in question here. The first is the initial diachronic change itself ("the rupture of the system's equilibrium"); the second is the manner in which the system is altered to absorb the

---

against the excessive domination of historicism in modern thought. The requirement of ever more exact and scientific approximation to the eternal stream of Becoming remains in force, only the question arises how we may unite the examination of fields with that of Becoming itself. If the structure of a field is visible only in the pure being of a motionless state of speech (or one conceived as motionless), if only linguistic and conceptual groups and the interdependence of meanings are to be considered, then history can come into being only as the comparison of static moments, as a description that moves discontinuously from one cross-section to each other, ever taking as its object the total field, ever comparing it to earlier and later configurations of the same object. It would depend on the density of the juxtaposed cross-sections to what degree one could ultimately approximate the actual stream of becoming itself. That real time can never actually be conceptualized in itself is a defect which this method shares with every other one, even with the purely historical method that finds its starting point in the individual word, so that it cannot honestly serve as a reproach. . . ." Jost Trier, *Der deutsche Wortschatz im Sinnbezirk des Verstandes* (Heidelberg, 1931), p. 13.

15 In Troubetskoy, *Principes de phonologie,* p. 334. The notion of a mutation may, however, itself be considered contemporaneous with Saussure's concept of synchrony, for it did not gain currency until its rediscovery by de Vries in 1900 (see Gertrude Himmelfarb, *Darwin and the Darwinian Revolution* [New York, 1959], pp. 268ff).

change (it is for this alteration that Jakobson apparently reserves the term "mutation"). Clearly, therefore, this solution only postpones the problem and shifts it to another level. No doubt the initial phonetic change is itself comprehensible in terms of historical events, migrations, or by reference to physiolinguistic laws of various kinds. But, as in our example from Dutch history, such explanation constitutes a borrowing from a different causal series, and the ultimate ground of the change still falls outside phonemics and into the realm of the diachronic and the purely phonetic, and remains, as such, meaningless in purely synchronic (Jakobson says "teleological") terms. Thus, although the diachronic model implicit in Saussure, the theory of mutations, is capable of giving a complex and suggestive picture of historical change, it does not in the long run manage to solve the basic problem of reuniting diachrony together with synchrony *within a single system*. Indeed, the very word "mutation," borrowed as it is from the older evolutionary model, stands as a symptom of the increasing contradictions of the Saussurean model when pushed to its outer limits.

That this contradiction is already present in Saussure himself can be judged from a close examination of one of his most famous images: language as a game of chess. The first extended comparison[16] is a straightforward one used to illustrate the idea of "system." In general the game itself, with its rules, is a synchronic system; its origins in Persia, or the replacement of a lost ivory chessman with a checker— none of these various external events has any bearing on synchrony. Only when the rules themselves are modified are we in the presence of a genuine synchronic event within the system. Yet in the second illustration[17] it is the succes-

---

[16] *Cours de linguistique générale*, p. 43.
[17] *Ibid.*, pp. 125-126.

sive positions of the pieces on the board, the successive moves, which are compared with the various synchronic moments of a language in evolution. Clearly, this analogy, satisfying historically because it makes of the successive synchronic states a kind of meaningful continuity, is not at all in the spirit of Saussurean thinking, for in the chess game, the rules remain the same throughout: whereas in the evolution of a language, it is precisely the rules that change. Saussure himself knows this so well that he indeed is ultimately embarrassed by his own analogy: "In order for the chess game to resemble the game of language at every point, one would have to suppose an unconscious or unintelligent player"—a sentence we may reverse by saying that precisely the analogy as stated tends to imply that diachronic changes in language are somehow meaningful, "teleological," in themselves, moves made by some meaningful force immanent in phonetic history.

2

The distinction between synchronic and diachronic is only the enabling act which permits Saussure's doctrine to come into being in the first place. No doubt it is a-historical and undialectical in that it is based on a pure opposition, a set of absolute contraries, which can never be resolved into any kind of synthesis. Yet once we grant it as a starting point, and move inside the synchronic system itself, we find that matters are there quite different. Here the dominant opposition is that between the *langue*, which is to say the ensemble of linguistic possibilities or potentialities at any given moment, and the *parole*, or the individual act of speech, the individual and partial actualization of some of those potentialities. It is instructive to examine the comments of Ogden and Richards on this distinction, for nowhere else is the difference between the two modes of thought so strikingly illustrated: "De Saussure does not pause at this point to ask himself what he is looking for, or whether there is any reason why there should be such a thing. He proceeds instead in a fashion familiar in the beginnings of all sciences, and concocts a suitable object— 'la langue,' the language, as opposed to speech. . . . Such an elaborate construction as *la langue* might, no doubt, be arrived at by some Method of Intensive Distraction analogous to that with which Dr. Whitehead's name is associated, but as a guiding principle for a young science it is fantastic. Moreover, the same device of inventing verbal entities outside the range of possible investigation proved fatal to the theory of signs which followed."[18]

A passage of this kind makes clear that what Ogden and Richards really object to in Saussure is precisely the dialectical quality of his thought. The vice of Anglo-American empiricism lies indeed in its stubborn will to isolate the object in question from everything else, whether it be a material thing, an "event" in Wittgenstein's sense, a word, a sentence, or a "meaning."[19] (This mode of thought, going back as it does to Locke, is, I believe, ultimately political in inspiration; and it would not be difficult, following the lines pursued by Lukács in *History and Class Consciousness* for rationalizing and universalizing thought, to show how

[18] *The Meaning of Meaning*, pp. 4-5.

[19] See, for instance, Wittgenstein, *The Blue and Brown Books* (New York, 1958), p. 42: "The sentence has sense only as a member of a system of language; as one expression within a calculus. Now we are tempted to imagine this calculus, as it were, as a permanent background to every sentence we say, and to think that, although the sentence as written on a piece of paper or spoken stands isolated, in the mental act of thinking the calculus is there—all in a lump. The mental act seems to perform in a miraculous way what could not be performed by any act of manipulating symbols. Now when the temptation to think that in some sense the whole calculus must be present at the same time vanishes, there is no more point in *postulating* the existence of a peculiar kind of mental act alongside of our expression."

23

such thinking is characterized by a turning away of the eyes, a preference for segments and isolated objects, as a means to avoid observation of those larger wholes and totalities which if they had to be seen would force the mind in the long run into uncomfortable social and political conclusions.)

Saussure's opposition is dialectical in that it involves a tension between a part and a whole either of which is inconceivable without the other: being relational rather than substantialist, it thus strikes directly at the kind of isolation of a single apparently free-standing element (such as a "statement") foreseen by empirical thinking. But even the defense of Saussure's "imaginary construct" must be dialectical, for clearly the initial logical problem is grounded, not in Saussure's terminology, but in the thing itself. It is precisely *because* language is the kind of peculiar entity that it is—nowhere all present at once, nowhere taking the form of an object or substance, and yet making its existence felt at every moment of our thought, in every act of speech —that the word which names it will not be able to function with the neatness of nouns that stand for physical objects. (The parallel with the concept of society is one which naturally imposes itself: Adorno has shown[20] how the antinomies in the idea of society result from the contradictions in the thing itself rather than from some inherent failure in conceptualization. In any case, this parallel is itself one of the reasons Saussure's model has in its turn seemed so suggestive to other disciplines.)

The opposition has another meaning as well, one which Ogden and Richards do not seem to have grasped, and which has crucial methodological implications. The new opposition is a different one from the first, although it uses

[20] T. W. Adorno, "Society," *Salmagundi*, Nos. 10-11 (Fall 1969-Winter 1970), pp. 144-153.

the same terms and amounts to a different dimension of the same basic reality; and although such terminological uncertainty has often been attributed to the hesitations in Saussure's thought, to the various stages at which the collated courses and lectures were given, and the unfinished, imperfectly systematic nature of this posthumous doctrine, I myself tend rather to attribute it to the relational character of his work in general. As we have seen above, the definition of the basic units of language—word, sentence, sign, phoneme, syntagma—is much less important than the grasping of relationship in a given concrete case. This is not to say that Saussure's thought dissolves into the unverifiable like an Empsonian ambiguity, but rather that its precisions hold only for the specific contexts under examination. In this sense, I do not think that the unfinished character of his work was accidental; he never could have finished it in any traditional sense: in this, as in so much else, in his modesty of personal bearing and the immeasurable range of the work he proposed himself, resembling Mallarmé.

The relationship of part to whole reflects an older logical model, that of the organism, which is no longer useful in the solving of the new kinds of problems posed by the peculiar nature of language. Thus the new form of the opposition will have as its function the untangling from one another of various heterogeneous systems within language itself. The *parole*, for instance, the individual act of speech, is irrelevant for Saussure's science not only to the degree that it is always, and of necessity, incomplete, but also insofar as it is the locus of individual difference, of individual personality and style. To see the relationship of *parole* to *langue* as member to class, however, or as part to whole, as physical event to physical law, would be to reintroduce the positivistic models of the Neo-Grammarians which it had precisely been Saussure's intention to replace.

25

His solution to this dilemma is ingenious: one may call it situational, or even phenomenological, in that it takes into account the concrete structure of speech as a "circuit of discourse," as a relationship between two speakers. It is this circuit which we ordinarily forget, when common sense suggests that the relationship of *langue* to *parole* is something inside ourselves, in the individual consciousness, a relationship between the immediate sentence I happen to have pronounced, and my power to construct sentences, my interiorized store of linguistic forms in general. Yet it is possible to break the circuit of discourse in a different place and to come up with a more methodologically suggestive model. This is the originality of Saussure, who separates the *parole* of the speaker from the *langue* of the person who understands him, for whom *parole* is the active, *langue* the passive dimension of speech, for whom indeed, as the Soviet linguist Smirnitsky has perceived,[21] *langue* is not so much the power to speak as it is the power to understand speech. Thus, at one stroke, all purely articulatory matters, all questions of local accent, mispronunciation, personal style, are eliminated from the new object under consideration, becoming themselves problems for a different science, that of the *parole*. The study of the *langue* remains concrete, for we can investigate it by testing the limits and characteristic forms of any native speaker's understanding; yet the investigation is now no longer complicated by the presence of some particular object (like an individual sentence) to which it would stand as a physical law to its experimental manifestation.[22]

[21] N. Slusareva, "Quelques considérations des linguistes sovietiques à propos des idées de F. de Saussure," *Cahiers Ferdinand de Saussure*, Vol. xx (1963), pp. 23-41.

[22] The originality of Chomsky's transformational grammar seems to derive from a reversal of the Saussurean model, a kind of negation of the negation in which the linguistic mechanisms are relocated back in the *parole* or individual act of speech. See Chomsky's comments

The theoretical advantages of this new model can be measured if we compare it to what seems to have been its source in the sociology of Durkheim.[23] Not only does the latter's insistence on the representational nature of social facts strongly resemble Saussure's notion of signs (to be examined shortly); but the very thrust of Durkheim's thought, in its attempt to separate out the personal and individual from the objective and social, is quite consistent with the Saussurean distinction between *langue* and *parole* which we have just been examining. Only Durkheim, in order to assure a methodological foundation for his research, is led to posit the existence of a collective consciousness of some kind which underlies the collective representations, just as the individual consciousness does for the individual ones. Clearly this hypothetical entity merits the kind of criticism we have seen Ogden and Richards mete out to Saussure, in its suggestion of an organic group existence of some kind. But note that where Durkheim must have recourse to an imaginary collective substance, the very peculiarity of Saussure's object, which is the circuit of discourse, permits him to escape any such substantialist illusion, even as a methodological hypothesis. The objection of Ogden and Richards is inappropriate in Saussure's case, for the very construction of his model excludes consideration of any "collective mind"[24] and indeed forces the attention in wholly

---

on Saussure: "He was thus quite unable to come to grips with the recursive processes underlying sentence formation, and he appears to regard sentence formation as a matter of *parole* rather than *langue*." (Noam Chomsky, *Current Issues in Linguistic Theory* [The Hague, 1964], p. 23.)

[23] See W. Doroszewski, "Quelques remarques sur les rapports de la sociologie et de la linguistique: Durkheim et F. de Saussure," *Journal de psychologie*, Vol. xxx (1933), pp. 82-91; and also Robert Godel, *Les Sources manuscrites du cours de linguistique générale de F. de Saussure* (Geneva, 1957), Addendum, p. 282.

[24] It is only fair to point out that the expression "esprit collectif"

different and unrelated directions. It is for this reason also, I think, that the Saussurean model has become more useful for social scientists than that of Durkheim, whose false problems it permits them to avoid.

It is instructive to gauge the originality of this model against yet another projection, namely that which we find in literature, where the application of the idea of the circuit of speech in "Folklore as a particular type of artistic creation" by Jakobson and Bogatyrev yields instructively different results from Sartre's analysis of the role of the public in *What Is Literature?* For Sartre, the other term of the circuit of discourse, the public, is implicit in the writer himself, and follows logically from the choices of material and the stylistic formulations which are the acts of his own solitude. This is not a psychological identification; or, rather, Sartre's analysis takes place on a level which excludes psychology as such, for it merely shows how a certain selection of material, involving a lengthy presentation of certain things and only the most schematic references to others, as though they were already immediately intelligible to his audience, is in itself a selection of the readership, as a group possessing certain social characteristics, certain familiarities, certain types of knowledge. His illustration is black literature, which will clearly vary in style and tone as it is addressed to the in-group itself, or to white people, to whom so many allusions, so much that is unfamiliar, has first to be explained. Thus the model of Sartre is a relatively individualistic and Kantian one, in which the nature of the individual's relationship to groups outside or to society can be determined by internal analysis of the degree to which his own attitudes and ideas constitute a kind of universality.

---

does figure twice in the *Cours de linguistique générale* (pp. 19 and 140), where it has however no real philosophic significance.

Jakobson and Bogatyrev, on the other hand, follow the Saussurean model in their investigation of the relationship of individual creation and individual style to those collective and anonymous objects which are folk tales. No doubt everything in the folk tale originates with the individual, just as all sound changes must; but this necessary fact of invention in the first place is somehow the least essential characteristic of folk literature. For the tale does not really become a folk tale, given the oral diffusion of this literature, with its obvious dependence on word of mouth circulation, until the moment when it has been accepted by the listeners who retain it and pass it on. Thus the crucial moment for the folk tale is not that of the *parole*, that of its invention or creation (as in middle-class art), but that of the *langue*; and we may say that no matter how individualistic may be its origin, it is always anonymous or collective in essence: in Jakobsonian terminology, the individuality of the folk-tale is a redundant feature, its anonymity a distinctive one.

Yet in spite of the suggestiveness of this new distinction between *langue* and *parole*, it is clear that the problem of the relationship of part to whole will return in it in one form or another, if only in the relationship between my understanding of an individual sentence and my power to understand in general. In other words, it is now necessary to go more deeply into the concrete ways in which the *langue* is articulated into a system.

3

We may find a first clue to the nature of these articulations by once more contrasting the terminology of Ogden and Richards with Saussure's equivalents. Where the former, as semanticists, are concerned with words as symbols, the latter is insistent on the definition of language as a system of signs. It is perhaps difficult at first glance for a layman

29

to understand the immense fortune which this Saussurean term has known, not only among linguists, but in other projections as well. Once again, however, the quality of the innovation is clear only against the background of that which is being changed by it.

Saussure's definition of the sign runs as follows: "The linguistic sign unites, not a thing and a name, but a concept and an acoustic image,"[25] the latter terms being then replaced by a new set, the "signifié" and the "signifiant," the signified and the signifier. The point is made further that the sign is wholly arbitrary, that its meaning rests entirely on social convention and acceptance and that it has no "natural" fitness in and of itself.[26]

Thus, the very construction of the concept of a sign allows us as it were to read backwards through it the various earlier theories it was designed to replace. For one thing, it clearly strikes down the most archaic language theory of all, one still occasionally revived by poets, that of the indissoluble link between words and things, which is to say the apprehension of language as names and naming. There can no longer be any question of such an intrinsic relationship once the utterly arbitrary character of language has been made clear. Far more fruitful from the poetic point of view, is the reversal of this older doctrine by Mallarmé, for whom

[25] *Cours de linguistique générale*, p. 98.

[26] The word "natural" is not Saussure's but was added by his editors (see Leroy, *Les Grands courants de la linguistique moderne*, pp. 106-108). Émile Benveniste's influential critique of Saussure's doctrine of the "arbitrary" nature of the sign (in "La Nature du signe linguistique," *Problèmes de linguistique générale*, pp. 49-55) has always seemed to me both true and misleading. The relationship is of course not arbitrary for the speaker but rather for the analyst himself; and the doctrine of the arbitrary character of the signifier seems to me to play an essential enabling and functional role in Structuralism in general (witness Derrida's doctrine of the trace!), one which, as we shall see below, corresponds roughly to the hypothesis of the unconscious in psychoanalysis.

poetry comes into being, not as an attempt to restore the old Adamic names, but rather in reaction against this arbitrary quality of language and as an attempt to "motivate" that which in its origin was wholly "unmotivated": "Les langues imparfaites en cela que plusieurs, manque la suprême: penser étant écrire sans accessoires, ni chuchotement mais tacite encore l'immortelle parole, la diversité, sur terre, des idiomes empêche personne de proférer les mots qui, sinon se trouveraient, par une frappe unique, elle-même matériellement la vérité. Cette prohibition sévit expresse, dans la nature (on s'y bute avec un sourire) que ne vaille de raison pour se considérer Dieu; mais, sur l'heure, tourné à de l'esthétique, mon sens regrette que le discours défaille à exprimer les objets par des touches y repondant en coloris ou en allure, lesquelles existent dans l'instrument de la voix, parmi les langages et quelquefois chez un. A côté d'*ombre*, opaque, *ténèbres* se fonce peu; quelle déception, devant la perversité conférant à *jour* comme à *nuit*, contradictoirement, des timbres obscur ici, là clair. Le souhait d'un terme de splendeur brillant, ou qu'il s'éteigne, inverse; quant à des alternatives lumineuses simples—*Seulement, sachons n'existerait pas le vers*: lui, philosophiquement rémunère le défaut des langues, complément supérieur."[27]

Thus the doctrine of the arbitrariness of the sign eliminates the myth of a natural language. At the same time it serves to throw psychological considerations of language onto a different plane as well: for now what distinguishes human beings is no longer that relatively specialized skill or endowment which is the power to speak, but rather the more general power to create signs; and with this, the royal road from linguistics to anthropology is thrown open.

But there is still more: the force of the Anglo-American

[27] Stéphane Mallarmé, *Oeuvres complètes* (Paris, 1945), pp. 363-364.

terminology, of the word "symbol," was to direct our attention towards the relationship between words and their objects or referents in the real world. Indeed, the very word "symbol" implies that the relationship between word and thing is not an arbitrary one at all, that there is some basic fitness in the initial association. It follows that for such a viewpoint the most basic task of linguistic investigation consists in a one-to-one, sentence-by-sentence search for referents, and in the purification from language of non-referential terms and purely verbal constructs. The bent or twist of this model leads straight to Basic English, common language philosophy, and semantics as an organized discipline. Such an approach underestimates the weight of sheer historical convention and inertia in language at the same time that it overestimates the importance of "lack of communication" and of the so-called language barrier in human events.

Saussure, on the other hand, is deflected by his very terminology from the whole question of the ultimate referents of the linguistic sign. The lines of flight of his system are lateral, from one sign to another, rather than frontal, from word to thing, a movement already absorbed and interiorized in the sign itself as the movement from the signifier to the signified. Thus, implicitly, the terminology of the sign tends to affirm the internal coherence and comprehensibility, the autonomy, of the system of signs itself, rather than the constant movement outside the symbol-system towards the things symbolized which we find in Ogden and Richards. Just as the latter implies semantics as its ultimate field of study, so the former points ahead to semiology as its ultimate fulfillment.

The philosophical suggestion behind all this is that it is not so much the individual word or sentence that "stands for" or "reflects" the individual object or event in the real world, but rather that the entire system of signs, the entire field of the *langue*, lies parallel to reality itself; that it is the totality of systematic language, in other words, which is analogous to whatever organized structures exist in the world of reality, and that our understanding proceeds from one whole or Gestalt to the other, rather than on a one-to-one basis. But, of course, it is enough to present the problem in these terms, for the whole notion of reality itself to become suddenly problematical; and indeed, for semiology, the latter is either a formless chaos of which one cannot even speak in the first place, or else it is already, in itself, a series of various interlocking systems—non-verbal as well as verbal—of signs.

4

We must now determine the manner in which the individual signs are related among each other, for it is this mode of relationship which will make up the linguistic system as a whole. The starting point must clearly be the realm of sounds, the material dimension of language. But if we remember the distinction insisted on both by Saussure and his spiritual contemporaries in the Slavic world—that between "pure" sounds and acoustic images, between measurable but meaningless sonorities and those which organize themselves into a kind of perceptual pattern for us—then the way in which to pose the problem is given. At what point do sounds become acoustical images? What does it take for phonetic matter to be transformed into a phonemic organization or system?

Thus posed, the question contains its own answer, for the shift involved is indeed a perceptual one, and presupposes an abandonment of an atomistic, empirical perception of an isolated thing-in-itself, a sound-object that has no connection with anything else, for a relational type of perception, something on the order of the Gestalt perception of form against field, or the dialectical tension between part and whole. Yet the latter formulations are not the appropriate ones in this case, for it is the relationship to the opposite rather than to the whole which marks this kind of organization.

The acoustic image of signifier is made up of a series of differential or distinctive features. Our perception of a given phoneme is a differential perception, which is to say that we cannot identify a word as a singular masculine noun without at the same time apprehending it as *not* being a plural, or a feminine word, or an adjective. This type of simultaneously identifying and differentiating awareness holds true all the way down to the smallest meaningful units of the word, namely the phonemes and their particular distinctive features.

Thus language perception follows in its operation the Hegelian law that determination is negation; but it is perhaps Sartre's distinction between internal and external negations which makes its specificity clearest. External negation obtains in analytical thought, and in the world of physical objects juxtaposed side by side. Thus, to say that a table is not a giraffe is to say something true, but non-essential, which affects neither the being of the table nor that of the giraffe, which in other words does not really contribute to the definition of either. But human reality is governed by the internal negation; so that the fact that I am not an engineer, or a Chinese, or a sixty-year-old, says something that touches me profoundly in my very being. So with language: each sound stands in a relationship of internal negation to the other elements of its system.

One may characterize the peculiar reality of language by saying that for it the concepts of difference, distinction, and opposition, which in other fields of thought do not always imply each other, here fall together and are all one and the same. The movement of Saussure's thought may perhaps be articulated as follows: language is not an object, not a substance, but rather a value: thus language is a perception of identity. But in language the perception of identity is the same as the perception of difference; thus every linguistic perception holds in its mind at the same time an awareness of its own opposite.

R-chords.

Although distinctive features can attain combinations of great complexity, the most basic form they can take is that of a series of binary oppositions. The simplest form of such oppositions, and at the same time the most profoundly dialectical, is a tension between presence and absence, between positive and negative (or zero) signs, in which one of the two terms of the binary opposition "is apprehended as positively having a certain feature while the other is apprehended as deprived of the feature in question."[28] Here most clearly the difference between phonemic and phonetic perception is demonstrated: for the first, nothing is present at all (in other words, the non-Russian-speaker listening to Russian is not even aware of what might have been present in the way of sounds); for the second, a determinate absence is heard, is felt. What is at stake is the difference between not-being itself and absence as a Gestalt organized around some central emptiness.

Perhaps for the layman nothing illustrates the dependence of the mind on such binary oppositions so well as the apparent exception, in which our differential perceptions click on and off in the void. Thus, by thinking the words "fish" and "sheep" rapidly over, first in the singular and then in the plural, the mind can be felt instinctively to work up a feeling of opposition where none is physically or materially present.

[28] Troubetskoy, *Principes de phonologie*, p. xxvii.

Saussure's idea of the system has known its most complete practical application in the science of phonemics, particularly in the works of Trubetskoy and Jakobson. At the same time, one must point out that the more specialized a field of investigation becomes, the more a general linguistics risks breaking into separate and unrelated units, and the more endangered becomes Saussure's insistence on the unity of language as a phenomenon. We may say this in another way by pointing out that there is a difference between this type of binary opposition, and what ordinarily passes under the name of opposition in dialectical thought and which would be more properly described as a contradiction. The former is a static antithesis; it does not lead out of itself as does the latter. In this sense one may wonder whether a system can be generated out of what remain discrete pairs, whether it can become anything but, in the Jakobsonian terminology, a "bundle" of pairs, an additive grouping of oppositions under the sign of eternal negation. Indeed, I believe that the static structure of the binary opposition is merely another form taken, within the system, by the initial antithesis which was Saussure's starting point, and which here returns, reinteriorized, to set a limit on the dynamism for which it was in the beginning responsible.

5

But there is yet another aspect of Saussure's description of the system which we have not yet taken into account. The level now described is no longer that of the individual sounds and sound patterns but rather the larger dimension of what in traditional grammar used to be called syntax, that of the word and the sentence. This older terminology is, of course, no longer adequate, since, as we have seen, it presupposes fixed units of measurement, substantialist concepts of stable entities, which neither correspond to the fluid nature of language nor offer a purely formal structure through which the latter may be revealed. But just as we were able before to characterize the mode of perception (identity and difference) of the units we no longer felt able to define in themselves, so now, in the necessary absence of any adequate definition of the sentence or of the parts of speech, we are still able to characterize their way of being together, the forms their combinations take.

For Saussure, the signs or units of meaning tend to form two different general kinds of relationships: the syntagmatic and the associative (which, for symmetry and following the glossematicians, we may call the paradigmatic). The syntagma is a horizontal grouping, a succession of meaning-units or words in time. The sentence is therefore one form which the syntagma can take, and in it the relationships governing the units are references backwards and forwards in time. Thus the verb "reflects" refers us back to a subject, at the same time that it anticipates an ultimate object as well; in an uninflected language like English, a noun tends to imply for the mind the imminence of a verb.

At the same time, however, the word "reflects" carries in itself another, we might call it a vertical, dimension. For it makes us think of the other words with which we associate it, the noun "reflection" for instance, and any other words formed on the same stem; the verb "deflect" and any other words rhyming with it or having a similar internal organization; and hosts of other associations as innumerable, indeed, as are the types of sentence or syntagma that might be formed around the verb taken as a horizontal entity.

We recognize here once again, in disguised form, the primary Saussurean distinction between the diachronic (the temporally successive, horizontal dimension) and the synchronic (the simultaneous and systematically organized vertical one). And as in the *Cours de linguistique générale*

37

as a whole, so also in this particular problem of the priority of the two modes of relationship, it is clear that Saussure's bias is for the synchronic, for the associative or paradigmatic, as against the diachronic or the syntagmatic. The logical priority of the former is already implicit in the model; for it seems clear that the only way the mind can feel the verbal, syntagmatic function of a word like "reflects" is to bear within itself paradigms of the sentence as a whole, to have already learned, by the associative chain, the verbal function and operation in general.

The syntagmatic dimension, in other words, looks like a primary phenomenon only when we examine its individual units separately; then they seem to be organized successively in time according to some mode of temporal perception. In reality, however, we never perceive them separately: the "verb" is always felt to be part of a larger unity, which is the syntagma itself, and which now, since it is no longer a series of units but rather a unity of its own, is reabsorbed into associative thought and understood through its resemblance to other syntagmata.

What is involved is the basic distinction between contiguity and similarity, the two basic principles of the association of ideas already implicit in the classic discussions of Locke, Hume, and Kant. Such distinctions are classificatory ones, and aim ultimately at the discovery and formulation of absolute mental laws, of the ultimate patterns and categories according to which the mind, and indeed the brain, work.

In any case, it seems to me that if the theory of binary organization reflected the initial starting point of Saussure's thought formally, as the act of creating an opposition, the present distinction between associative and syntagmatic modes reflects the content of that initial opposition, which, at first outside the system and permitting it to come into being, is now reinteriorized and recurs within the synchronic domain itself. Now it becomes problematical to what degree the object of study is the thought pattern of the linguist himself, rather than that of language, and we here more clearly perceive the moment in which the originality of Saussure's point of departure returns to limit his results: for that initial repudiation of history, which at the very outset resulted in an inability to absorb change into the system as anything but a meaningless and contingent datum, is now reproduced, at the very heart of the system itself, as an inability to deal with syntax as such.

Such are the distinctive features of Saussure's doctrine as a whole, and with the completion of this rapid sketch we take leave of official linguistics. Is it necessary to add that our attitude towards this material is of a wholly different type than that of the linguist himself? Where the latter is intent on the referent, on the object named by the various Saussurean theories, our own interest has been the coherence of the system as a whole in its own right, and its suggestiveness as a model or analogy for other modes of thinking. The linguists have gone on to work Saussure's system through to its logical conclusions, and indeed, with Chomsky, to reverse it, proposing a new linguistic model altogether. We, however, will henceforth be concerned with the afterlife of the original theory in other realms of knowledge, and in particular with its liberating influence, as model and analogy, in the areas of literary criticism, anthropology, and ultimately of philosophy itself.

39

II

The Formalist Projection

THE UNIQUE claim of the Russian Formalists is their stubborn attachment to the intrinsically literary, their stubborn refusal to be diverted from the "literary fact" to some other form of theorization. Thus, whatever the ultimate value of their systematic thinking, literary criticism cannot but start where they started, and the most consequent Marxist attacks on them, such as those of Trotsky and Bukharin never denied this initial methodological validity.[1]

The Formalists began, as did Saussurean linguistics, with the isolation of the intrinsic itself, with the disentanglement of their specific object of study from those of the other disciplines, with a systematic examination of what Jakobson called *literaturnost* (literariness), the distinguishing element of literature itself. This procedure is already dialectical in that it does not foresee any particular type of content dictated in advance, but rather seeks empirically to identify whatever specific dominant elements the individual work of art proposes, a process of identification which can be successfully completed only in correlation with the other elements of the work and indeed of the period itself. Such a definition of the central elements of the work is therefore a relational or functional one, and depends fully as much on an awareness of what the element is not, of what has been omitted from the work in question, as of what the element is. Thus the object of study of the Formalists may be plot or image-structure, but it may also be the epigraphic habit

[1] See Leon Trotsky, *Literature and Revolution* (New York, 1957), p. 180: "The methods of formal analysis are necessary but insufficient." Except for names and titles already in print, Russian words have throughout been transliterated according to the Library of Congress system without diacritical marks.

43

of the nineteenth-century novelists, or the name scheme of their characters: whatever starting point happens to meet the eye, to foreground itself, to push itself forward insistently into the field of perception. In this way the method begins by warning against itself and against its own too mechanical application.

As with Saussurean linguistics also, the first moves of the Russian Formalists had to be negative, and were aimed at disentangling the literary system from other extrinsic systems. These attacks and polemics can be sorted out into three general categories: (1) those on the idea of literature as the bearer of a philosophical message or of philosophical content; (2) those which attempt to analyze literature genetically, or, as we would now say, diachronically (biographically, through a study of sources, etc.), as in Alexander Veselovsky's attempt to show the origins of various motifs of the folk-tale in religious rituals and primitive beliefs, wherein the work is dissolved into heterogeneous elements analyzed from a non-literary point of view[2]; and, finally, (3) in the polemic against what is perhaps the most "literary" of these positions, the tendency to resolve the literary work into a single technique or a single psychological impulse—here the Formalists have in mind a formula

[2] See Eichenbaum, "The Theory of the 'Formal Method,'" in *Literatura (Teoria, Kritika, Polemika)* (Leningrad, 1927), p. 129, or in *Russian Formalist Criticism: Four Essays*, trans. Lee T. Lemon and Marion J. Reis (Lincoln, Nebraska, 1965), p. 117: "Veselovsky explained epic repetition as a mechanism for the original performance (as embryonic song). But an explanation of the genetics of such a phenomenon, even if true, does not clarify that phenomenon as a fact of literature. Veselovsky and other members of the ethnographic school used to explain the peculiar motifs and plots of the *skaz* by relating literature and custom; Shklovsky did not object to making the relationship but challenged it only as an explanation of the peculiarities of the *skaz*—he challenged it as an explanation of a specifically literary fact. The study of literary genetics can clarify only the origin of a device, nothing more."

like that of Belinsky, for whom poetry is "thinking in images."

(In a narrow sense this third target is part of an attack by the Formalists on the preceding generation, dominated by Symbolism. But in a broader way it is directed against all undialectical literary research, all literary analysis which as naively as pre-Socratic philosophy seeks to isolate some ultimate and changeless element beneath the multiplicity of literary appearance: some ultimate essence of literature, whether irony or metaphor, paradox or peripety, tension, *Erhabenheit*, "high seriousness," or whatever.)

The American New Critics share only the first two of these three polemic aims. Since they have so often been compared with the Formalists, it is perhaps well to recall some basic differences. Clearly enough the two movements reflect a more general historical shift in the literary and philosophical climate with the passing of the nineteenth century. This shift, often described as a reaction against Positivism, varies according to the composition of the national and cultural situation in which it takes place, and according to the character of the dominant ideology against which the younger writers rebel.

Thus, while both the American and the Russian critical movements are contemporaneous with a great modernistic literature, although both arise in part as an attempt to do theoretical justice to that literature, the Formalists found themselves to be contemporaries of Mayakovsky and Khlebnikov, revolutionaries both in art and in politics, whereas the most influential literary contemporaries of the American New Critics were called T. S. Eliot and Ezra Pound. This is to say that the familiar split between avant-garde art and left-wing politics was not a universal but merely a local, Anglo-American phenomenon.

45

Yet even this is itself but the reflection of a more profound historical and cultural divergence between the two movements. The New Critics, following mentors like Irving Babbitt and Charles Maurras, explicitly repudiated English Romanticism and its radical tradition and returned for their models to Metaphysical and Cavalier poetry. The Formalists, however, merely attacked the utilitarian and social tradition of the criticism of Pushkin and his generation, reserving the latter as a privileged object for their own characteristic type of literary analysis and reevaluation. Thus the Formalists are rather inclined to reclaim for their own purposes, rather than to renounce, this great formative period in Russian literature, one characterized by political as well as literary upheavals, in which most of the great writers were in sympathy with the abortive Decembrist revolt, "that famous pause in Russian history on the square in front of the Petersburg Senate."[3]

Such sympathy has formal consequences for literary criticism as well: the privileged narrative models available to the New Critics were the Elizabethan verse drama and Dante's *Commedia*. For them, therefore, the specific problems of narration are blurred and mingled with more properly verbal or poetic problems: what is analyzed is the moment in which a character comes to poetic speech, or in which in Dante a situation or a destiny is suddenly fulfilled and crystallized in a single verse. Pushkin, however, is the inventor both of modern Russian poetry and of modern Russian story-telling, not just of verse and of its transposition to a poetic art prose of some kind, but of two wholly different literary modes, each of which follows its own intrinsic formal laws. The example of Pushkin is therefore ever present to the Formal-

[3] Yury Tynyanov, *Death and Diplomacy in Persia* (London, 1938), p. 224.

ists as a double lesson: that verse and prose narration follow rigorously different laws, but that in another sense these laws, that of poetic language or syntax, and that of prose narration or plot, may be thought of as forming parallel and analogous, although wholly dissimilar, systems. At any rate, in all these ways, in their attitudes toward history, in their attitudes towards literary history, and in their attitudes towards that internal literary diachrony which is narration and plot, the Formalists may be seen to have a far more positive and dialectical attitude than the American New Critics.

Not that the Russian Formalists can be thought of as having a single position, a single literary doctrine; yet their work was a collective one, and possesses a unity of development in time. "The *Opojaz* [Society for the Investigation of Poetic Language]," Tomashevsky tells us, "never was a regularly constituted group with a list of members, a meeting place, laws. Yet during the most productive years it had an appearance of organization in the form of a kind of committee of which Viktor Shklovsky was president, Boris Eichenbaum his aide-de-camp, and Yury Tynyanov the secretary."[4] Like other literary schools, the German Romantics or the Surrealists, the Opajaz seems to have developed a doctrine of *Geselligkeit* to justify its own collective unity. Shklovsky himself has much in common with the directors of other literary movements in analogous moments of fusion and formation, with Pound, with Friedrich Schlegel, with Breton: a union of seminal ideas, intellectual impudence, and a fragmentary artistic performance which results in the canonization of the fragment as a genre, whether explicitly in Schlegel and in the Surrealists' discontinuous view of

---

[4] Boris Tomashevsky, "La Nouvelle école d'histoire littéraire en Russie," *Revue des études slaves*, Vol. viii (1928), p. 227, n. 1.

lived experience; or implicitly in the ideogrammatic practice of the *Cantos*, and in Shklovsky's single-sentence paragraphs and deliberate interpolation of heterogeneous anecdotes and materials. At the same time, the idea of the Opajaz or the Formalist group of critics, is itself a narrow and misleading one, inasmuch as Shklovsky also worked closely with Mayakovsky and later on with Eisenstein, and was, along with other Formalists, closely associated with the novelists of the "Serapion Brothers group," whose literary practice reflects Formalist ideas. Thus an ultimate evaluation of Formalism as a concrete literary phenomenon will bring it much closer to genuinely creative movements such as German Romanticism or Surrealism than to a purely critical doctrine like that of the American New Criticism.

Shklovsky's own doctrine is both the starting point for Russian Formalism and the source of its own internal contradictions. We will see how a coherent literary theory was impossible without Shklovsky's initial contribution, and at the same time ultimately workable only at the price of eliminating the distinctive marks left on it by Shklovsky's personality.

1

1. The initial task of the theory is the isolation of the specifically literary fact itself. The title of Shklovsky's most important book, *The Theory of Prose*, serves as a manifesto: a theory of poetry already having been developed, the intention is to break new ground, to apply what has been discovered about poetry to a hitherto unexplored domain, namely the short story and the novel itself. The theory of poetry had been based on an absolute separation of poetic language from the language of everyday communication, a distinction already formulated by Mallarmé in a characteristic economic figure:

"Un désir indéniable à mon temps est de séparer comme en vue d'attributions différentes le double état de la parole, brut ou immédiat ici, là essentiel.

"Narrer, enseigner, même décrire, cela va et encore qu'à chacun suffirait peut-être pour échanger la pensée humaine, de prendre ou de mettre dans la main d'autrui en silence une pièce de monnaie, l'emploi élémentaire du discours dessert l'universel *reportage* dont, la littérature exceptée, participe tout entre les genres d'écrits contemporains."[5]

The Formalists began by demonstrating that in many ways poetic speech stood to everyday language as a type of dialect, governed by its own peculiar laws, indeed often even pronounced differently (as in the sounding of the mute *e*'s, the aspiration of the initial *h*'s at the *Comédie française*). The deeper implication is that poetry is not merely a specialized part of everyday language, but constitutes a total linguistic system in its own right.

In Anglo-American criticism the model used for the separation of literary from ordinary language is based on a presupposition as to the nature of rationality, and turns on the distinction between cognitive (or referential) and emotional speech. The endless and rather futile debates on the relative value of art and science are therefore already implicit in this starting point, which gives science the edge by the very force of its terminology.

With the downgrading of epistemology, however, the dis-

---

[5] Mallarmé, *Oeuvres complètes*, p. 368. Such a separation, however, apparently only isolates poetics from linguistics by distinguishing the object of the former from the object of the latter. In reality, it is precisely this initial starting point, which, making of poetic speech a determinate type of linguistic utterance in its own right (rather than a decoration, a primitive stage of language, or whatever), reintegrates the study of poetic speech into linguistics itself. The work of Roman Jakobson is the most striking proof of such a unity (see below pp. 202-203).

49

tinction between rational and irrational, cognitive and emotional modes, no longer seems as absolute as it once did. Phenomenology, and the existential thought that comes out of phenomenology, discards the distinction as an artificial separation, and takes its starting point precisely in the notion of the act of consciousness, in terms of which both emotions and ideas are modes of being-in-the-world. Indeed, the bias of existentialism may be said to be rather towards emotion and feeling (Heidegger's *Stimmung*) as concrete experiences and away from the abstraction of pure knowledge.

Thus where an older epistemological philosophy tended under its own momentum to imply the primacy of knowledge, and to relegate other modes of consciousness to the level of emotion, magic, and the irrational, the inherent tendency of phenomenological thought is to reunite them under the larger unity of being-in-the-world (Heidegger) or of perception (Merleau-Ponty). It is in this kind of philosophical atmosphere that the Formalist ideas of language must be understood.

2. A poetic language which is a dialect is one which attracts attention to itself, and such attention results in renewed perception of the very material quality of language itself. The new model in terms of which the Formalists will develop their theory is therefore based on the opposition between habituation and perception, between mechanical and thoughtless performance and a sudden awareness of the very textures and surfaces of the world and of language. Such an opposition, which goes beyond the conventional one of action and contemplation, of the practical and the perceptual, clearly shifts the burden of proof from literature as a concrete mode of being-in-the-world to the abstractions of the sciences.

Shklovsky's famous definition of art as a defamiliarization, a making strange (*ostranenie*) of objects, a renewal of perception, takes the form of a psychological law with profound ethical implications. The passage from Tolstoy's journals which Shklovsky quotes in illustration is as close as he ever comes to taking an actual metaphysical or ethical position: "I was cleaning a room and, meandering about, approached the divan and couldn't remember whether or not I had dusted it. Since these movements are habitual and unconscious, I could not remember and felt that it was impossible to remember—so that if I had dusted it and forgot —that is, had acted unconsciously, then it was the same as if I had not. If some conscious person had been watching, then the fact could be established. If, however, no one was looking, or looking on unconsciously, if the whole complex lives of many people go on unconsciously, then such lives are as if they had never been."[6] Art is in this context a way of restoring conscious experience, of breaking through deadening and mechanical habits of conduct (*automatization*, as the Czech Formalists will later call it), and allowing us to be reborn to the world in its existential freshness and horror.

Yet such purely psychological laws as are here implied are not really of the same kind as those of Potebnya (art as metaphor, metaphor as a conservation of energies) which the Formalists attacked; the latter have a content, while the new psychological mechanism with which Shklovsky replaces them only circumscribes a form. The new concept of *ostranenie* is not intended to imply anything about the nature of the perceptions which have grown habitual, the perceptions to be renewed. Its peculiar usefulness for criticism lies in the way it describes a process valid for all literature

[6] Quoted by Shklovsky in "Art as Technique" (*Russian Formalist Criticism: Four Essays*), p. 12.

without in any way implying the primacy of one particular literary element (such as metaphor) or one particular genre over the others.

Ostranenie as a purely formal concept has three signal advantages, which go far towards explaining the paradoxical richness of Shklovsky's own practical criticism, essentially little more than an endless set of variations on this one idea. First, as we have seen, defamiliarization serves as a way of distinguishing literature, the purely literary system, from whatever other verbal modes there are. It thus serves as the enabling act which permits literary theory to come into being in the first place.

Yet at the same time it permits the establishment of a hierarchy within the literary work itself. Inasmuch as the ultimate purpose of the work of art is now given in advance —namely the renewal of perception, the seeing of the world suddenly in a new light, in a new and unforeseen way—the elements and techniques or devices (*priyomy*) of the work are now all ordered towards this end. The subsidiary devices turn out in Shklovsky's terminology to be the motivation of those essential devices which permit renewed perception in the first place. Thus in Tolstoy's *Kholstomer*, a great many aspects of social life are suddenly seen as somehow brutal and unnatural, and this essential unfamiliarity of the habitual is then motivated by the point of view of the story, which is observed, not through human eyes, but through those of a horse.

Finally, the notion of *ostranenie* has yet a third theoretical advantage in that it permits a new concept of literary history: not that of some profound continuity of tradition characteristic of idealistic history, but one of history as a series of abrupt discontinuities, of ruptures with the past, where each new literary present is seen as a break with the dominant artistic canons of the generation immediately preceding. It is a model of artistic history not unlike that proposed by Malraux in the *Voices of Silence,* except that where Malraux's theory is formulated in terms of the psychology of creation and the need for each successive generation to react against its own masters, the Formalists saw this perpetual change, this artistic permanent revolution, as being inherent in the nature of artistic form itself, which, once striking and fresh, grows stale and must be replaced by the new in unforeseen and unforeseeable manners.

At the same time, the Formalist model is more complicated than this hypothesis of perpetual change, and involves a complex system of mutations and readjustments not unlike Jakobson's model of diachronic linguistics. Literary evolution is not only a break with the dominant and existing canons; it is the canonization of something new at the same time, or rather the lifting to literary dignity of forms until then thought to be popular or undignified, minor forms until then current only in the demi-monde of entertainment or of journalism (think of the manner in which the detective story became the novel of Robbe-Grillet). To use a favorite image of Shklovsky, it is an eccentric movement, like the move of the knight in a chess game. "In the liquidation of one literary school by another," he says in a famous sentence, "the inheritance is passed down, not from father to son, but from uncle to nephew."[7]

Thus, from the basic notion of *ostranenie* an entire literary theory comes into being, first by the isolation of the

---

[7] Viktor Shklovsky, *O teorii prozy* (Moscow, 1929), p. 227 (or *Theorie der Prosa,* trans. G. Drohla [Frankfort, 1966], p. 164). Compare Shklovsky's *Sentimental Journey* (trans. Richard Sheldon [Ithaca, New York, 1970]), p. 233:
"New forms in art are created by the canonization of peripheral forms.
"Pushkin stems from the peripheral genre of the album, the novel from horror stories, Nekrasov from the vaudeville, Blok from the gypsy ballad, Mayakovsky from humorous poetry."

purely literary system itself; second by a model of the various relationships obtaining in that synchronic system; and, finally, as we have just seen, by a return to diachrony in the analysis of the kind of change which obtains from one synchronic state to another. Let us now evaluate these results, particularly as they bear on the question of time and history.

2

1. It is only fair to point out that the idea of art as a renewal of perception is not unique with the Formalists, but can be found in one version or another everywhere in modern art and modern aesthetics and is at one with the primacy of the new itself. Thus Proust, comparing the letters of Madame de Sévigné with the techniques of his impressionist painter Elstir, describes her style as follows:

"It was at Balbec that I realized how she makes us see objects the same way he does, following the order of our perceptions rather than explaining them first through their causes. But even that afternoon in the train, as I reread the letter about moonlight: 'I could resist the temptation no longer, I put on all my bonnets and veils, unnecessary as they are, I pace that mall, whose air is as sweet as in my own room; I find a thousand phantoms, black and white monks, nuns, several of them, grey and white, linen scattered here and there upon the ground, shrouded men leaning against the trees, etc.' I was enchanted by what a little later I would have called (for does not she depict her landscapes in the same way he does his characters?) the Dostoyevskian side of Madame de Sévigné's *Letters*."[8]

The implication that the abstract understanding (an explanation through cause-and-effect) is a kind of poor sub-

[8] Marcel Proust, *A la recherche du temps perdu* (Paris, 1954, 3 vols.), Vol. I, pp. 653-654.

stitute for perception, that there is a kind of interference between a purely intellectual knowledge of a thing and some genuine, spontaneous, visionary experience of it, is of course basic to the whole construction of Proust's novel. It is at the same time part of a general feeling in the modern world that life has become abstract, that reason and theoretical knowledge have come to separate us from a genuine existential contact with things and the world. This is true not only in literature but also in criticism: thus Proust resembles the Formalists in the above passage not only in what he says, but in his manner of saying it. It is already a defamiliarization to compare Madame de Sévigné with Dostoyevsky; the very shock has the effect of making us see her style in a new and utterly unforeseen light, as though for the first time.

2. Yet when we examine the objects perceived, we find that on the whole they tend to fall into two general groups. Thus Swift, motivating his device by the abbreviated size of Gulliver among the Brobdingnags, has his character make the following observations: "I must confess no Object ever disgusted me so much as the Sight of her monstrous Breast, which I cannot tell what to compare with, so as to give the curious Reader an Idea of its Bulk, Shape and Color. It stood prominent six Foot, and could not be less than sixteen in Circumference. The Nipple was about the Bigness of my Head, and the Hue both of that and the Dug so varified with Spots, Pimples and Freckles, that nothing could appear more nauseous: For I had a near Sight of her, she sitting down the more conveniently to give Suck, and I standing on the Table. This made me reflect upon the fair Skins of our *English* Ladies, who appear so beautiful to us, only because they are of our own Size, and their Defects not to be seen but through a magnifying Glass, where

we find by Experiment that the smoothest and whitest Skins look rough and coarse, and ill coloured."[9] Such a perception is basically a way of relating to nature itself, and may be said, in its loathing and horror before the natural, to constitute a relatively metaphysical vision, in what it forces us to notice about the very bodily conditions of human life itself.

During the same period, however, and particularly in France, analogous literary techniques of defamiliarization are being put to rather different political and social ends. We recall the Persians who visit the court of Louis XIV in the declining years of the latter's reign in Montesquieu's *Lettres persanes*, seeing its more grotesque and improbable aspects from the outside, without preconceptions. In the same way the various visitors from outer space or from the untouched forests of the new world in Voltaire's *contes philosophiques* prove to be more than adequate media for perceiving and enregistering the structural peculiarities of European life. The following passage from La Bruyère, however, somewhat earlier chronologically, may stand as the most striking example of such defamiliarization: "One sees certain ferocious animals, male and female, scattered over the countryside, black, livid, and burned by the sun, bound to the soil which they dig and turn over with unconquerable stubbornness; they have a sort of articulate voice, and when they stand up they exhibit a human face, and in fact they are men. They retire at night into dens, where they live on black bread, water, and roots; they spare other men the toil of sowing, tilling, and harvesting in order to live, and thus deserve not to be without the bread

[9] Jonathan Swift, *Gulliver's Travels* (in *Selected Prose Works* [London, 1949]), pp. 189-190. A useful historical survey of the techniques of defamiliarization (the author calls it "negative allegory") may be found in Dmitry Čiževsky, "Comenius' Labyrinth of the World," *Harvard Slavic Studies*, Vol. i (1953), esp. pp. 117-127.

which they have sown."[10] This horrifying text, one of the first explicit descriptions of the peasantry in modern French literature, no longer directs our attention to the natural and metaphysical conditions of human life, but rather to its unjustifiable social structure, which we have come to take for granted as something natural and eternal, and which therefore cries out for defamiliarization. This application of the techniques of *ostranenie* to the phenomena of social life is contemporary with the dawn of historical consciousness in general.

No doubt these two forms, the metaphysical vision and the social critique, are not as mutually exclusive as we have made out; very often, as in such a recent and striking example of the technique as Sartre's *Nausea*, they are interrelated, and we find examples of both.[11] Yet it is clear that each tendency moves to absorb the other to its own profit. Thus, in this early novel, the force of Sartre's critique of bourgeois society is blunted by his preponderantly metaphysical and apolitical vision of the absurdity of all human life. It is however equally clear that neither mode is ultimately reconcilable as a description with Shklovsky's concept of literature; for either implies the primacy of a certain type of content, either metaphysical or social. For Shklovsky, the latter is merely a pretext for the renewal of vision in any way possible: thus Swift's misanthropy is merely the "motivation" of his concrete technical effects on

[10] Quoted in Erich Auerbach, *Mimesis* (trans. Willard Trask [Princeton, New Jersey, 1968]), p. 366.

[11] Metaphysical: "I forgot it was a root. Words had vanished, and with them the meanings of things and their uses, all those feeble pointers that men had traced upon their surface. I was sitting hunched up, all alone with this knotty black utterly raw mass which frightened me" (*La Nausée* [Paris, 1962], p. 179). Social: "In the churches, by candle light, a man standing in front of kneeling women drinks wine" (*La Nausée*, pp. 63-64). For examples from Sartre's other works, see my *Sartre: the Origins of a Style* (New Haven, Connecticut, 1961).

a sentence-by-sentence basis; so is the social irony of Voltaire and Montesquieu; so is Sartre's ontology. The priorities are reversed; everything—personality, social consciousness, philosophy—exists to permit the coming into being of the literary work itself.

There is, however, yet another way to pose the problem; and it is particularly instructive to compare the theory of Shklovsky with that of Bertolt Brecht which bears the same name: the theory of the so-called "estrangement-effect" (where the German *Verfremdung* literally means estrangement, like Shklovsky's Russian equivalent). The originality of Brecht's theory was to have cut across the opposition between the social and the metaphysical in a new way, and to throw it into a completely different perspective. For Brecht the primary distinction is not between things and human reality, not between nature and manufactured products or social institutions, but rather between the static and the dynamic, between that which is perceived as changeless, eternal, having no history, and that which is perceived as altering in time and as being essentially historical in character. The effect of habituation is to make us believe in the eternity of the present, to strengthen us in the feeling that the things and events among which we live are somehow "natural," which is to say permanent. The purpose of the Brechtian estrangement-effect is therefore a political one in the most thoroughgoing sense of the word; it is, as Brecht insisted over and over, to make you aware that the objects and institutions you thought to be natural were really only historical: the result of change, they themselves henceforth become in their turn changeable. (The spirit of Marx, the influence of the *Theses on Feuerbach*, is clear.) At the same time, this genuinely historical vision returns even upon the metaphysical perceptions themselves, until then seemingly permanent, lending them also the value of an effect rather than a cause.

Thus, in this context, the passage of Swift quoted above would result from the social deformation of sexual desire and reflect its social character in the preference for fair skin, and so forth.

Shklovsky's doctrine itself, by seeing literary change as a uniform mechanism the same at all times and all places, no doubt keeps faith with the existential situation of literary production (for at any given point, there is really only one change that counts), but at the same time ends up turning diachrony into mere appearance and undermining any genuine historical awareness of the changing of forms. Yet, as we have seen, it is not hard to restore genuine history to Shklovsky's model if we turn our attention from the history of works to the history of perception itself, if we try to account for the specific types and determinate modes of mystification or of perceptual numbness which the individual work of art is an attempt to dispel.

3

1. The problem has yet another dimension, which involves what we may call internal, rather than external, diachrony. Alongside the question of the meaningful succession in time of the various concrete historical examples of defamiliarization in literature, there is the problem of the relationship, within a single work of art, of the defamiliarization technique to the movement and change of events and objects in time. Thus the opposition between poetry and prose reappears as a distinction between the making strange of a single simultaneous image and the treatment of a series of events, or in short of plot or narration itself.

It would seem that for Shklovsky the two processes are different only in their scope and not in their essential mechanisms. Both—the perception of an object and the perception of an action—involve a kind of lingering in time, a kind of handling and slow turning about on all sides: "Why does Ovid, who made an *Art of Love* out of love itself, advise us to take our pleasure in leisurely fashion? The path of art is a tortuous path, on which your feet feel each stone, a path that winds back and forth. Word goes together with word, one word rubs against the other like a cheek against another's cheek. Words are separated from words, and instead of a single complex, an automatically pronounced expression that shoots out like a chocolate bar from a dispenser, there comes into being a word as sound, a word which is purely articulated movement. Ballet similarly is movement which you feel, or better still, a movement so constructed that you have to feel it as such."[12]

Thus the techniques for plot defamiliarization and those of lyric are analogous, as macrocosm to microcosm. Better still, in an implied metaphor with language and with the sentence, one which will become explicit with the Structuralists, the basic way of seeing any object anew is "to place the object in a new semantic row, in a row of concepts which belong to another category."[13] This can be done by leaving off the name and merely describing the object in its empirical inertia; or by rendering it from some unusual angle, from over a great distance; or microscopically as in the passage from Swift quoted above; in slow motion, as with many of the gestures or indeed with the basic action itself in *Tristram Shandy*; by juxtaposing the object with a different object which causes hitherto unnoticed properties of the first to stand out sharply (Pound's ideograms); by tampering with conventional expectations of cause-and-effect (as in Sartre's analysis of fantastic literature); and so forth.

[12] *O teorii prozy*, pp. 24-25 (*Theorie der Prosa*, pp. 28-29).
[13] *O teorii prozy*, p. 245 (*Theorie der Prosa*, pp. 184-185).

Most, but not all, of these techniques can be transferred to narrative plot (the fable or *sujet*), where the principal categories of defamiliarization turn out to be retardation, composition by steps (i.e., decomposition of the action into episodes), double-plotting (including the interpolation of heterogeneous anecdotes and stories), and, finally, the "baring of the device" (the deliberate attracting of the reader's attention to the basic techniques of narration itself, a category in a somewhat different class from the previous ones, which we will consider by itself in the next section).

I hesitate to point out the degree to which these categories or techniques lose their strangeness when reformulated in cinematographic terms, where they are abundantly familiar as montage, cross-cutting, and so forth. There is for one thing something self-defeating in the attempt to recast a theory of defamiliarization in older, more habitual terminology; for another, it is just as likely that Eisenstein, from whom these concepts derive, was influenced in his theoretical speculations by Viktor Shklovsky, long a collaborator of his, rather than the other way around. What is mainly significant about the parallel with the movies as a narrative form is that it implies a preexisting separation between form and content. The "fable" of the movie is given in advance, either someone's idea, the book to be adapted, or indeed the footage already shot. Then it is edited, selected out, put together in the appropriate sequence. We will see shortly whether this initial internal separation implied by the very idea of a "technique" does not ultimately limit what Shklovsky can do with narration in general.

The problem is not unlike the one raised in connection with Saussurean linguistics. We have seen that Shklovsky can deal adequately with the basic literary unity in terms of something like the sign in language. For him, this is that moment in which a habitual perception is suddenly re-

61

newed, and we see a thing freshly in a kind of perceptual tension with our older mode of thinking about it, experiencing both identity and difference at the same instant. Yet after the problem of the sign comes the problem of syntax, and the question is hardly a specious one, particularly if we recall Lukács' notion that narration is our basic way of coming to terms with time itself and with concrete history.

2. The problem of plot is thus not solved by the above enumeration of techniques or devices. There remains the second and more difficult question of their organization, the ultimate question, in short, of the totality of the work: "What is necessary in order for a story to strike us as *complete*?"[14] To put it another way, one of the basic requirements for any theory of plot must be that it contain some means of distinguishing that which is not plot, that which is incomplete, that which does not work. An adequate definition must function negatively as well as positively, just as the theory of generative grammar is required to reject non-sentences as well as to produce genuine ones.

In this context Shklovsky's attention to non-stories, such as the unfinished anecdotes in Le Sage's *Diable boiteux*, is revealing, for it allows us to try out different versions of the same anecdotal material, to feel which versions sound complete and which fall flat. Thus, for instance, the addition of a final atmospheric landscape picture to Gogol's *Ivan Ivanovich & Ivan Nikiforovich* completes what might otherwise have seemed as pointless as an anecdote in Lesage. Indeed, it seems to me that it is at this price that such concepts as that of qualitative progression, developed by Kenneth Burke or Yvor Winters,[15] cease to be mere classifica-

---

[14] *O teorii prozy*, p. 63 (*Theorie der Prosa*, p. 63).
[15] See Kenneth Burke, "Lexicon Rhetoricae," in *Counterstatement* (Chicago, 1953), pp. 123-183, and Yvor Winters, "The Experimental School in American Poetry," in *In Defense of Reason* (New York, 1947), pp. 30-74.

tory concepts or moral judgments and win genuine structural value.

Yet if the various devices of defamiliarization resembled the relationship of words to expected or unexpected contexts, if narrative sequence is in general something like a sentence, it would be more accurate to say that for Shklovsky the completed narrative, the story that works and has a point, is analogous to word play. For the tying up or unravelling of the knot is like the coincidence of two verbal series in the pun. It is like popular etymology in reverse, and Shklovsky shows how a good many primitive stories originate as a form of popular etymology (how such-and-such got its name, and so forth). Deceitful prophecies or oracles ("if Croesus attacks the Persians, a mighty empire will fall!") have a similar function in their unexpected resolutions, which strike the mind as a combination of two heterogeneous series; many fairy tales are also constructed along these lines (the unexpected solving of a riddle, performing of an unperformable task). On the most abstract level one may define such plot-resolution as an appearance of multiplicity (involving at least two semantic rows) suddenly and unexpectedly reunited back into unity: the word "unexpected," however, which may seem to be the operative one, is in reality already given in advance within the definition, for we must first be convinced of the initial resistance, the initial multiplicity, and at that point any prestidigitation which brings unity out of it will perforce be unexpected by us.

The resolution need not, however, be completely spelled out: "A special form is that of the story with the 'negative ending.' Yet first I'd like to explain this term. In the words *stola, stolu,* the vowels *a* and *u* constitute the endings and the root *stol-* the stem. In the nominative singular the word *stol* has no ending, yet in comparison with other forms of the declension we perceive this absence of an ending as the sign of a case: we can call it a 'negative form' (a term of Fortunatov) or in Baudouin de Courtenay's terminology a 'zero degree.' We find these negative forms very often in the short story, particularly in those of Maupassant. For example: a mother visits her illegitimate son, who has been brought up in the country. He has become a loutish peasant. In despair, she runs off and falls in the river. The son, not knowing who she is, poles the river and fishes the body out. The story ends at that point. Unconsciously the reader perceives the story against the background of the traditional story that does have an 'ending.' Moreover (but this is more an opinion than a thesis) the French novel of manners at the time of Flaubert very often uses the technique of the uncompleted action (as in *L'Éducation sentimentale*)."[16]

3. It is as an analysis of plot that we may examine one of the richest Formalist investigations, *The Morphology of the Folk Tale* of Vladimir Propp. Propp's initial stimulus is not unlike Shklovsky's in that he reacts against the treatment of isolated content in folk-tales, in particular against the Aarne system of the classification of motifs,[17] in which tales are separated according to whether their principal characters are animals, ogres, magical figures, humorous figures, and so forth. He does not have much trouble showing that a given story may be the same whether the figure in question is a wolf, a dragon, a witch, an ogre, or even an object of some kind.

Thus Propp establishes a distinction between horizontal and vertical which is a little like the Saussurean categories of the syntagmatic and the associative on the one hand, and

---

[16] *O teorii prozy*, pp. 73-74 (*Theorie der Prosa*, pp. 68-69).
[17] See, for a description of the Aarne classification, Stith Thompson, *The Folktale* (New York, 1967), pp. 413-427.

the Shklovskian distinction between the basic device (the actual defamiliarization) and the motivation on the other. The story line is considered as a series of abstract functions; the form taken by the various functions—the shape and identity of a given character or a landscape, or the nature of the obstacles—is unessential and derives its content from the cultural and historical context. It is like the concept of motivation insofar as the character of Baba Yaga would be an adequate justification for malignancy in the eyes of a Russian audience, where listeners from another culture would more adequately understand a dragon, a troll, or whatever.

Let us look more closely at Propp's basic story line, this long winding molecule of episodes which reminds one of a twelve-tone row, or, to anticipate Structuralist tendencies, some complex code patterned into the brain cells themselves. The basic tale begins with either injury to a victim, or the lack of some important object. Thus, at the very beginning, the end result is given: it will consist in the retribution for the injury or the acquisition of the thing lacked. The hero, if he is not himself personally involved, is sent for, at which point two key events take place.

He meets the donor (a toad, a hag, a bearded old man, etc.), who after testing him for the appropriate reaction (for some courtesy, for instance) supplies him with a magical agent (ring, horse, cloak, lion) which enables him to pass victoriously through his ordeal.

Then, of course, he meets the villain, engaging him in the decisive combat. Yet, paradoxically enough, this episode, which would seem to be the central one, is not irreplaceable. There is an alternate track, in which the hero finds himself before a series of tasks or labors which, with the help of his agent, he is ultimately able to solve properly.

65

Propp underscores the mutually exclusive character of these two sequences: either a villain or a series of tasks, but not both at once.[18]

The latter part of the tale is little more than a series of retarding devices: the pursuit of the hero on his way home, the possible intrusion of a false hero, the unmasking of the latter, with the ultimate transfiguration, marriage and/or coronation of the hero himself. Propp's own research ends with the establishment of this basic chain of episodes, which is to that degree an empirical discovery, and has the force of an existing fact.[19] I think, however, that given a formal point of view, which aims at determining how a particular story is felt to be complete, it will not be difficult to draw a few more general conclusions.

No doubt, as we have pointed out, the ending of the story is already implicit in its beginning (injury → retribution, lack → acquisition), so that it would seem to be enough for the story to proceed to its own ending and then stop. This abstract schema is, however, not that of the story or anecdote, but of the wish-fulfillment. It is enough to reflect on the pointlessness, the almost ungeneralizable individuality, of the wish-fulfillment as something told or communicated to realize that as such it can only be a non-story; that, although the structure of the wish may be a necessary precondition for the coming into being of a story, it is not a sufficient one.

At this point, we may recall Arthur Danto's definition of historical narration, as any form of "causal" explanation of how a given state of affairs A turned into a given state of

---

[18] Vladimir Propp, *The Morphology of the Folk Tale* (Austin, Texas, 1968), pp. 101-102 and 108-109.

[19] Hence Propp's comment on Shklovsky's proposition that the "tale is collected and laid out according to laws still unknown." "This law," he observes with finality, "has been determined." (*Morphology of the Folk Tale*, p. 116, n. 6.)

affairs *B*. The type of causal explanation used is important only in the sorting out of the various types or genres of history: theodicy, chronicle, ethical history, economic history, history as the deeds of great men, and so forth. The center of gravity of the narrated events lies not in the fact of the change, but in the explanation of the change, in the middle term which modulates from one state to the other (and Danto explicitly assimilates this to the dialectical process).[20] In this light it becomes clear what is lacking in the abstract schema of the folk-tale which we have given: the donor. The donor is therefore the element which explains the change described in the story, that which supplies a sufficiently asymmetrical force to make it interesting to tell, and which is therefore somehow responsible for the "storiness" of the story in the first place. Thus, the satisfaction and the completeness of the tale comes not from the fact that the hero manages to rescue the princess in the end, but rather from the means or agent given him to do so (a bird who tells him the right word to say to the witch, a magic cloak that lifts him to the tower, and so forth). This is to say something a little more than that what interests us in a story is the how rather than the what: what Propp's discovery implies is that every How (the magical agent) always conceals a Who (the donor), that somewhere hidden in the very structure of the story itself stands the human figure of a mediator, even in those more sophisticated forms in which he is concealed beneath more rational motivation.

We may restate the necessity for the existence of a donor in yet another way by pointing out the fact that in the beginning the hero is never strong enough to conquer by himself. He suffers from some initial lack of being: either he is simply not strong enough or not courageous enough, or

[20] Arthur C. Danto, *The Analytical Philosophy of History* (Cambridge, England, 1965), pp. 236-237.

67

else he is too naive and simple-minded to know what to do with his strength. The donor is the complement, the reverse, of this basic ontological weakness.

So it is that in the folk-tale, in the hero's story, an Other is implied, but not quite where we expected to find it: not in the form of the princess, for she can be replaced with a ruby or a feast or any other desirable object (and indeed she is basically herself little more than a desirable object, a combination of sensual beauty and the possibility of wealth and power); not in the form of the villain either, for reasons we will examine shortly. The basic interpersonal and dramatic relationship of the narrative tale is therefore neither the head-on direct one of love nor that of hatred and conflict, but rather this lateral relationship of the hero to the ex-centric figure of the donor.[21]

When we come now to the problem of the villain, it seems to me that the solution is given in that equivalence and mutual exclusion of the two systems which Propp stresses without interpreting it: the implication being that we are dealing with two modes of a single phenomenon, two faces of the same basic situation, which can take the form either of malignant threats and injury from a conscious agency or of a series of difficult and perplexing tasks. Interpersonal competition or work: Sartre's *Critique de la raison dialectique* has, I think, given us the clue to this equivalence, which reflects the primary reality of a world of scarcity, a world in which not only can I not fulfill my own basic needs without work, but in which my very existence is a threat

[21] René Girard's hypothesis (in *Mensonge romantique et vérité romanesque* [Paris, 1961], trans. *Desire, Deceit, and the Novel* [Baltimore, Maryland, 1965]) that in modern society desires are not natural but learned, that the story the novel tells is the learning of desire from some mediator or third party, can be reformulated in terms of the donor and of his ontological support of the hero as it is here described.

to the existence of others as well.[22] There is a basic Manichaeism of the world of scarcity, and it is scarcity which causes the Other to appear before me as a primal enemy. This alternance and indeed equivalence of back-breaking labor and of intense distrust and hostility to the stranger or the Other in general is what the narrative sequences of the fairy tale reflect. It is worth recalling in this context Ernst Bloch's idea that where myths reflect the warriors and the priesthood, the fairy tales are the narrative expressions of the poorer classes.[23] (Clearly, in more sophisticated art products more complicated combinations are possible. Thus, in the medieval romance, the alternate sequences of a set of tasks and of the struggle with the Other are united in the institution of the tournament.)

4. What I have tried to show is that the empirical discovery of a given set of functions cannot constitute an adequate explanation of the folk-tale as form, as completed narrative.[24] Just as we have shown how the syntagmatic dimension in Saussure, the horizontal sequence of functions in the sentence, tended to be reabsorbed into the associative or synchronic dimension, in which a sentence was understood as just one manifestation of the countless other possible manifestations of a given syntactical formation or unit, so here also it would seem that there can be no genuine law of the story or of the folk-tale unless the diachronic sequence of narrated events, the syntax of narration, is somehow transposed into a synchronic structure. This is what the rather Hegelian analysis we have given of Propp

[22] See my *Marxism and Form* (Princeton, New Jersey, 1971), esp. pp. 233ff.

[23] See "Zerstörung, Rettung des Mythos durch Licht," in *Verfremdungen*, Vol. i (Frankfurt, 1963).

[24] This is essentially the critique of Lévi-Strauss in "La Structure et la Forme," *Cahiers de l'Institut de science économique appliquée*, No. 99 (March, 1960).

aims at doing—reducing the individual events to various manifestations of some basic idea, such as that of otherness, or of work, and ultimately reducing those ideas to some central notion on which they are all partial articulations, so that what at first seemed a series of events in time at length turns out to be a single timeless concept in the process of self-articulation.

This almost spatial unity was already implicit, in a different form, in Shklovsky's plot analyses, and in the very idea of defamiliarization that underlay them. Defamiliarization was originally a method derived from lyric or at least lyrical perceptions, and in its application to plot it retains traces of its relatively more static origins.[25] Only pre-existing things—objects, institutions, units of some kind—can be defamiliarized; just as only what has a name to begin with can lose its familiar name and suddenly appear before us in all its bewildering unfamiliarity. The abundant examples of the technique which Shklovsky finds in Tolstoy do not therefore really tell us anything about the novel as a form, for they are fragmentary and static perceptions and rely on that which is already conventionally given in Tolstoy's society. Thus opera can be shown to be peculiar and improbable, unreal, only on condition that we are already familiar with it as a conventional institution and because we already take it for granted. So with all the other possible objects of *ostranenie*: battle (Stendhal, Tolstoy), marriage

[25] It is only fair to point out that for Shklovsky perception as such is not static but dynamic: "To make an object into an *artistic* fact, it has to be removed from the series of real-life facts. To do that you have to 'put it in motion' the way Ivan the Terrible 'passed his troops in review.' You have to tear the thing from the row of habitual associations in which you find it. You have to rotate it like a log in the fire" (*O teorii prozy*, p. 79 [*Theorie der Prosa*, p. 75]). Yet it is precisely this movement inherent in the static perception of lyric which in the present context allows the movement of the story's events to be assimilated to it.

(*The Kreutzer Sonata*), middle-class etiquette (*Nausea*), work (Chaplin's *Modern Times*). The fact that we have names for these objects indicates that we already, in advance, think about them in a unitary, atemporal way, as objects of one kind or another.

Thus synchronic thought secretly reintroduces itself back into the study of diachrony. It is for this reason, I think, that Shklovsky's method is incapable of dealing with the novel as such, and applies only to the short story. He was never able to view the novel as anything but a syncretic form, an artificial amalgamation. In this respect the essay on *Don Quixote* is particularly revealing. In it Shklovsky sets out to demolish the "myth," the "philosophical content," of Don Quixote himself. The novel does not exist, he shows us convincingly enough, in order to project this figure; rather, the figure of Don Quixote is invented and gradually elaborated in order to hold together the plot and to lend a unity to what would otherwise fall apart into a collection of unrelated anecdotes and episodes. (So in a similar way we might say that Hamlet's madness is a technical device designed to hold Shakespeare's various plot strands, derived from heterogeneous sources, together in an apparent surface unity; thus what looks like content turns out to be motivation.) As true as this may be, it comes with all the force of that genetic criticism which Shklovsky had just devoted his energies to refuting: for the origins of *Don Quixote*, its "making," ought not to have anything to do with its unity and with whatever makes it feel like a complete thing.

We may put this in a somewhat different way by saying that Propp's study lacks a generic dimension. It nowhere includes the possibility of defining the form of the folk-tale, its essential "laws," in terms of those other forms which it is not; or indeed of opposing the very concept of a form with laws to that of one which structurally lacks them. Lévi-

Strauss, in his series of *Mythologiques,* is more consequential when he feels the need to come to terms with narrative objects on the very border line between myth and something else, objects which have already begun to empty of their "internal organizational principles. The structural content [of such narrative substances] is dispersed. For the vigorous transformations of genuine myths we now find feeble ones substituted. . . . The sociological, astronomical and anatomical codes whose functioning we hitherto observed out in the open now pass beneath the surface; and structure sinks into seriality. This degradation begins when oppositions turn into mere reduplications: episodes succeeding each other in time, but all formed in the same pattern. It is complete when reduplication itself takes the place of structure. The form of a form, reduplication receives the dying breath of structure itself. Having nothing more, or so little, left to say, myth now survives only by repeating itself."[26]

It is significant that Lévi-Strauss correlates the transformation with a vaster changeover in the very feeling of temporality itself. The myth as a strict form thus proves to be the reflection of a solar periodicity which expresses itself in the longer rhythms of the year or the season; while the breakup of myth may be timed to the coming into being of a shorter lunar time, one which shows monthly or even daily rhythms. When we add to this the observation that Lévi-Strauss is as hostile to the novel as he is to the historical (or "hot") society from which the latter issues as a diachronic form, then it seems to me that we are able to form a more adequate picture of the relationship between synchrony and the strict formality of myth or folk-tale, and diachrony and the precarious formal solutions of the novel.

We may assume as axiomatic—in this for the moment

[26] Lévi-Strauss, *L'Origine des manières de table* (Paris, 1968), p. 105.

more faithful to the spirit of Lukács' *Theory* than to that of Shklovsky—that the novel as a form is a way of coming to terms with a temporal experience that cannot be defined in advance or indeed dealt with any other way. In a genuine novel, in other words, there cannot be any name for the basic subject matter in question; there cannot be any preexisting conventional substance on which defamiliarization is able to act. To put it another way, we can name only the things that happen to other people; our own lived experience, our existence, our feeling of the passage of time, are all too close to us to be visible in any external or objective way; they form the privileged object of the novel as narration, for it is at one with the evocation of just such incomparable, nameless, unique experiences and sensations.

It follows that there are no preexisting laws that govern the elaboration of the novel as a form: each one is different, a leap in the void, an invention of content simultaneous with the invention of the form. It is because the short story or the myth or tale, on the other hand, are characterized by a specific and determinate type of content that their laws can be the object of investigation. Thus law depends in some sense upon synchrony; and we have seen how short stories or folk-tales have a kind of atemporal and object-like unity in the way they convert existence into a sudden coincidence between two systems: a resolution of multiplicity into unity, or a fulfillment of a single wish. This is to say that where we can easily identify the non-story, that which fails to correspond to the intrinsic laws of the story as a form (just as we can identify the non-sentence), the novel has no opposite in this sense, for it is not a genre like tragedy or comedy, like lyric or epic, like the folk-tale or the short story, and the novels which do exist in the world are not exemplars of some universal, but are related to each other according to a historical rather than a logical and analytical

73

mode. (Those sub-varieties of the novel which do have laws—I am thinking, for instance, of the detective story or the historical novel—are evolutionary oddities and dead-end streets rather than illustrations of any general tendency.)

Yet another way to express this basic difference between the novel as a diachronic phenomenon and the tale as an embodiment of synchrony would be to recall the teachings of Poe, whose "Philosophy of Composition" has so much in common with Shklovsky's method of bracketting the work. For Poe, the lyric and the short story must be in their very essence short, must hold on a single page or take less than an hour's reading; and this is not an accidental but a substantive requirement. They are both, in a sense, ways of surmounting time, of translating a formless temporal succession into a simultaneity which we can grasp and possess; and if from this point of view the novel is unjustifiable, it is on account of the endless prospect of genuine time unfolding that it promises.

Yet Shklovsky's investigations of the short story are not altogether fruitless for a theory of the novel itself. They show us what it is the novel must negate; they help us see the novel as a way of surmounting and transcending its initial starting point in the anecdote. The novel may thus in this sense be said to be a short story cancelled and lifted up (*aufgehoben*) into a higher and more complex form, carrying the laws of the latter within itself as a kind of inner environment which the organism is called upon to negate. It is instructive to note how many great modern novels—*Ulysses* and *The Magic Mountain* come at once to mind—began by taking the form of a short story in the mind of their creator. At any rate it seems to me that it is only at some such price, at the cost of holding together in the mind such utterly distinct and even antithetical methods as those of Lukács in the *Theory of the Novel* and of Shklovsky in his *Theory of Prose*, that a genuinely dialectical concept of narration might be achieved.

The Formalists were, however, able to grasp at least one aspect of the novel's form correctly: that was its ending, the point at which *durée* and diachrony break off, and which can therefore momentarily be seized in synchronic terms. "The novel," says Eichenbaum in his essay on O. Henry, "is characterized by the presence of an epilogue: a false conclusion, a summary in which perspectives of the future are opened, or in which the subsequent destinies of the main characters are told (see Turgeniev's *Rudin*, or *War and Peace*). This is why it's natural for the twist ending to be so rare a phenomenon in the novel (and where you do find it, it is merely a sign of the influence of the short story itself). . . ."[27]

4

1. The above are some of the synchronic limitations built into the concept of *ostranenie*; there is also about it a profound ambiguity which we have not yet touched on. *Ostranenie* can apply either to the process of perception itself, or to the artistic mode of presentation of that perception. Even granting the nature of art as defamiliarization, it is never clear in Shklovsky's writings whether it is the content or the form itself which is defamiliarized. All art, in other words, seems to involve some kind of renewal of perception; but it is not true of all art forms that they attract attention to their own specific techniques, that they deliberately "bare" or reveal their own "devices." Moreover, it is at this point that description slips into prescription: given the perceptual model Shklovsky started with—its association of perception with defamiliarization on the one

[27] Tzvetan Todorov (ed. and trans.), *Théorie de la littérature* (Paris, 1965), p. 203.

hand, and motivation with habituation or inertia on the other—it is not hard to see why he leans towards an art in which the "motivation" is utterly suppressed, an art which takes itself for its own subject-matter, and presents its own techniques as its own content.

The archetype for such a self-conscious literature is Sterne's *Tristram Shandy*, which in a much-discussed sentence Shklovsky described as "the most typical novel in world literature."[28] I believe that above and beyond the impudence, this sentence is to be taken literally: *Tristram Shandy* is the most typical novel because it is the most novelistic of all novels, taking as its subject-matter the very process of story-telling itself. The degree to which narrative technique is the content of *Tristram Shandy* can be gauged by comparison with the conventional first-person novel in which there is a distinction between actor and author, between hero and memorialist, between "Marcel" and "Proust." In Proust, the intrusion of the author remains abstract; we never see this second, reflective "I" directly, because it is through his mind that we are looking at the younger figure. In *Tristram Shandy*, every time we try to concentrate on the time of the content, of the actual events narrated, the life of Tristram himself, the sentences lead us back to their own time, the time of their writing ("I am this month one whole year older than I was this time twelve-month; and having got, as you perceive, almost into the middle of my fourth volume—and no farther than to my first day's life— 'tis demonstrative that I have three hundred and sixty-four days more life to write just now, than when I first set out; so that instead of advancing, as a common writer, in my work with what I have been doing at it—on the contrary,

[28] *O teorii prozy*, p. 204 (*Russian Formalist Criticism: Four Essays*, p. 57).

I am just thrown so many volumes back")[29] and the time
of our reading ("It is about an hour and a half's tolerable
good reading since my uncle Toby rung the bell, when
Obadiah was order'd to saddle a horse, and go for Dr. Slop,
the man-midwife; so that no one can say, with reason, that
I have not allowed Obadiah time enough," etc.).[30]

Moreover, even when we are able to witness the content
directly, without such authorial interference, we are made
to realize the incommensurability of words to experience,
of models to lived existence, by the manner in which gestures are drawn out in slow motion until their microscopic
notation becomes intolerable, in which segments of events
are fragmented to the point where the infinite divisibility of
all human experience in time seems a demonstrable fact.[31]
In such wise *Tristram Shandy* may be considered the first
dialectical picture of models: showing how reality can be
infinitely expanded or contracted, depending on the way it is
told; holding between the two infinites of the "life" that you
name and sum up in the title, and the pure "instant" which
is the last indivisible unit of narratable human time itself.

Tristram Shandy thus takes its place, for the Formalists,
as a predecessor of modern or avant-garde literature in general: of that "literature without subject-matter" of which
Shklovsky takes Rozanov as his exemplar, but with which

---

[29] Laurence Sterne, *Tristram Shandy* (New York, 1935), p. 191.
[30] *Ibid.*, p. 67.
[31] E.g., "As my father's India handkerchief was in his right coat
pocket, he should by no means have suffered his right hand to have
got engaged: on the contrary, instead of taking off his wig with it, as
he did, he ought to have committed that entirely to the left; and
then, when the natural exigency my father was under of rubbing his
head, called out for his handkerchief, he would have had nothing
in the world to have done, but to have put his right hand into his
right coat pocket and taken it out;—which he might have done without any violence, or the least ungraceful twist in one tendon or muscle
of his whole body." (*Ibid.*, p. 105.)

we are familiar enough as the plotless novel in general (indeed, Shklovsky uses the word "sujet" as the general equivalent of plot). Rozanov illustrates the resolution of the novel back into its raw materials, into a kind of linguistic collage, made up of journal entries, newspaper clippings, letters, entries noted on stray envelopes and scraps of paper, and so forth. From the point of view of content, he may be seen as a kind of Russian equivalent of Pirandello or Fernando Pessoa, with his multiple personalities (he was a conservative columnist under his own name for the *Novoe Vremya*, a liberal columnist under a pseudonym for the *Russkoe Slovo*). It is worth noting that for Shklovsky, even this ideological content is not primary, but only the result of the form which calls it into being: " 'Yes' and 'no' stand together on the same sheet of paper—a biographical fact is lifted to the rank of a stylistic one. The 'black' Rozanov and the 'red' one are there for artistic contrast, as is the opposition between the 'dirty' and the 'pure' Rozanov."[32]

It is hardly necessary to observe the ways in which Shklovsky's own literary practice follows this program: the memoir-like raw materials, with their interpolated stories, their digressions, their authorial interventions; the history of these works as deliberate collations of various manuscripts at various times in Shklovsky's life; the style, a kind of fragmentation into paragraphs, heavily relying on the newspaper-like shock of the one-sentence paragraph ("the 'style' of Viktor Shklovsky," complained Gorky, "the short and dry, the paradoxical phrase"),[33] the silences of understatement and ironic restraint, already a devaluation of "content" within the content itself. In the light of these works, one is tempted to consider the doctrine of defamiliari-

---

[32] *O teorii prozy*, pp. 234-235 (*Theorie der Prosa*, p. 173).
[33] Richard Sheldon, *Viktor Borisovič Shklovsky: Literary Theory and Practice, 1914-1930* (Ann Arbor, Michigan, 1966), p. 50.

zation itself as a kind of "motivation" for Shklovsky's own particular techniques.

We have called this slippage from defamiliarization in the content to defamiliarization in the form an ambiguity in Shklovsky's thinking, but it is not clear whether the ambiguity is an inadvertent or a deliberate one. Certainly the key sentence of the *Theory of Prose* leaves the matter more in doubt than ever: "Art is a means of re-experiencing the making of objects, but objects already made have no importance for art."[34] Are we to assume that all forms of art exist only to "bare their own devices," only to give us the spectacle of the creation of art itself, the transformation of objects into art, their being made art? (But in that case, only so-called "modern" art has any value, or rather even traditional art is really secretly modern for Shklovsky in its essence.) Or are we to assume some more metaphysical implication, namely that the very act of perception is itself a making of the object in question, and that to re-perceive an object anew is in a sense to become conscious of our own "making" activity? One is reminded, in that context, of Vico's doctrine that man only understands what he has made. But, characteristically, Shklovsky does not conclude; he is temperamentally allergic to metaphysical assertions.

2. It is instructive to compare this ultimate form which defamiliarization takes for Shklovsky in the "baring of the device" with the irony of the German Romantics, which in many ways resembles it. Romantic irony is something far vaster in its implications than the conventional authorial interventions associated with the term. For the most part, indeed, such interventions are merely drawn back into the content and reabsorbed in it: the work of art, immaterial, cannot be rent or wounded, but heals over again effortlessly

---

[34] *O teorii prozy*, p. 13: "Iskusstvo est sposob perezhit delanie veshchi, a sdelannoe v iskusstve ne vazhno."

without a trace, and the intervening "author" becomes simply one character or persona among others.

The larger concept of irony is at one with the general spirit of idealism itself, and Friedrich Schlegel explicitly appeals to contemporary science to justify it. It involves the gradual obliteration of Vico's distinction between history (which man, having made, can understand) and nature (which, as the result of God's creation, is utterly alien to us); the gradual feeling that we share in the non-human as well, or rather that the I and the not-I are subsumed together under some greater more all-encompassing entity on the order of a transcendental ego or an absolute spirit; that human consciousness therefore rediscovers seeds of itself in everything that it contemplates. Of this metaphysical idealism, then, the work of art clearly becomes the tangible symbol: not so much in the way its author reveals himself through the surface of creation, but precisely in the way in which he is concealed behind it, as half-veiled presence, half-transparent opacity:

> The immeasurable height
> Of woods decaying, never to be decayed,
> The stationary blasts of waterfalls,
> And in the narrow rent at every turn
> Winds thwarting winds, bewildered and forlorn,
> The torrents shooting from the clear blue sky,
> The rocks that muttered close upon our ears,
> Black drizzling crags that spake by the way-side
> As if a voice were in them, the sick sight
> And giddy prospect of the raving stream,
> The unfettered clouds and region of the Heavens,
> Tumult and peace, the darkness and the light—
> Were all like workings of one mind, the features
> Of the same face, blossoms upon one tree. . . .[35]

[35] Wordsworth, *The Prelude*, Book Six, vv. 624-637.

Irony thus characterizes our relationship to the work of art insofar as, knowing that the surface before us is an imaginary representation and the result of someone else's labor, we nonetheless consent to lose ourselves in it as though it were real, a state halfway between hallucination and cold, unamused withdrawal. In the same way, irony governs our relationship to the external world, for there is something paradoxical about an object, or a world in general, which is by definition external inasmuch as we have to have a relationship to it, but which is at the same time of the same substance of ourselves insofar as we can have a relationship to it.

The Surrealists, with their notion of *le hasard objectif* and their feeling for the ruses of desire—the way it crystallizes itself in the fascinating objects of the outside world, the way the unconscious projects itself into the signs and bric-a-brac of that immense *marché aux puces* which is the industrial landscape—are perhaps the closest formally to this older romantic idea.

By comparison Shklovsky's doctrine seems to have more in common with artisanal production. Like Pound, his insistence on technique seems to reflect a nostalgia for an older handicraft culture; his premium on technical know-how to be a way to give art and literature the solidity of a manual skill, like cobbling or pottery. (If further proof were necessary, one would have only to look at his pride at his technical performance in an armored car division in World War I, or at his glee at showing up Maxim Gorky's faulty knowledge of flax cultivation later in the twenties.) [36] If there seems an occasional similarity between Formalist analyses and Aristotelian literary methods, it is indeed to be attributed to this common model of art as craft or skill.

The same shift in emphasis from the ontological to the

[36] *Sentimental Journey*, p. 270; Sheldon, *Viktor Borisovič Shklovsky*, p. 51.

technical can be witnessed in the kind of emphasis placed on folk materials, crucial to both Romanticism and Formalism alike. The juxtaposition of the Grimms and Propp is here emblematic, for the recourse to the folk-tale, to the popular imagination, stands in both for the return to something elemental and original in the strictest sense; but for the Romantics this something was diachronic, where for the Formalists it was structural: the original language, the original sources of story-telling, as opposed to the fundamental structures of discourse and basic laws of plot revealed in their ultimate simplicity. For the spirit of the Formalist enterprise, imagine the New Critics with collective enthusiasm taking apart the nursery rhymes of Mother Goose!

3. The originality of the Formalists' idea of technique is to be found in its inversion. For Aristotle and the neo-Aristotelians, everything in the work of art exists for some ultimate purpose, which is the characteristic emotion or peculiar pleasure of the work itself as an object consumed. For the Formalists everything in the work exists in order to permit the work to come into being in the first place. The advantage of this approach is that whereas ultimately the Aristotelian analyses end up outside the work (in psychology and the extra-literary problems of the conventionality of emotion), for Shklovsky such emotions as pity and fear are themselves to be considered constituent parts, or elements of the work in the first place. Take the following discussion of feelings in *Tristram Shandy*:

"Sentimentality cannot be the content of art if for no other reason than that art has no separate contents in the first place. The representation of things from the 'sentimental point of view' is a special method of representation, similar to their representation from, say, the point of view of a horse (Tolstoy's *Kholstomer*) or from that of a giant (Swift).

82

"In its essence art is beyond emotion . . . unsympathetic—or beyond sympathy—except where the feeling of commiseration serves as material for the artistic structure. But even there, in considering the feeling one must consider it from the point of view of composition, just as in trying to understand a motor one must look at the drive-belt as a detail in a machine—from the mechanic's point of view—and not from the point of view of a vegetarian."[37]

This radical inversion of the priorities of the work of art is a critical revolution analogous to Saussure's disconnection of the referential, or to Husserl's bracketting in phenomenology; its intent is to suspend the common-sense view of the work of art as mimesis (i.e., possessing content) and as source or purveyor of *emotion*. The advantage of this bracketting is to constitute a system of intrinsically literary elements or facts: we saw how Aristotelianism tended to pass outside a purely literary system in the consideration of such problems as the normal psychological reaction of the suffering of a perfectly good man, or of a perfectly wicked man. In the same way, esthetic positions which presuppose content in the work of art tend to shift from the literary to the philosophical and social and lose sight of the purely literary functionality of a given fact in a literary work, whatever value the same element may have in another system.

Nowhere are the advantages of the Formalist position more apparent than in Boris Eichenbaum's classic essay on "The Making of Gogol's *Overcoat*," which he sees as an elaborate literary mimesis, as a transposition on the level of sophisticated artistic techniques, of the gestures and storytelling procedures of the traditional *skaz*, or oral yarn (the

---

[37] *O teorii prozy*, p. 192 (or "A Parodying Novel: Sterne's Tristram Shandy," trans. by W. George Isaac, in *Laurence Sterne: A Collection of Critical Essays*, ed. John Traugott [Englewood Cliffs, N.J., 1968], p. 79).

Russian equivalent, as the Formalists were fond of pointing out, of the American tall tale or the stories of Mark Twain). The techniques of the *skaz*—we would call their ensemble its style—are the primary element in this work, and we may summarize the paradoxical presuppositions of the method as follows. It is not because Gogol wishes to present a certain type of content that he appropriates to himself the style of the *skaz*. Rather, he wishes to create a literary style based on the *skaz*; he wishes to speak in a certain kind of voice, and, given that initial starting point, then looks around for the appropriate material, anecdotes, names, details, to use in it, to set it off properly, to allow the story-telling voice its full range of intrinsic effects. But if this is the case, then a number of hotly debated questions fall to the ground at once. There can, for instance, no longer be any question of a struggle between Romanticism and Realism in Gogol. The point is not to decide whether the "realistic" elements (St. Petersburg, poverty, the little people) take predominance over the grotesque or romantic elements (the ghost at the end, the character of Akaky Akakievich himself). Rather, the dominant style of the *skaz* requires both for its sudden alternations and contrasts. Moreover, the story is no longer fit for the propagation of philosophical or psychological truths. We can no longer speak of a literature of the common city people inaugurated by Gogol, or of the psychological innovations and insights transcribed by the author; these are little more than optical illusions of content, mirages of "truths" or "insights" given off by the operation of the artistic process itself.

In his essay on "Tolstoy's Crises" Eichenbaum extends his method even further, showing how in a sense Tolstoy's religious conversion itself could be considered a "motivation of the device," in the manner in which it provided new raw material for an artistic practice on the point of exhausting itself. (We have seen a similar inversion of priorities in Shklovsky's treatment of Rozanov.) It is perhaps inevitable that the inversion of the method, which began by denying the rights of psychological, biographical, and philosophical analyses, would end up absorbing them into it, drawing them, along with the author's entire life and experience, considered now as mere preparation for its production, back within the work of art itself.

With such bracketting, we are at the very heart of the Formalist method itself. This is perhaps the moment to express one's astonishment that in the fifteen years since the publication of Victor Erlich's definitive English-language survey of Formalism, this movement has had so little impact on American critical practice. Perhaps the habits of specialization run so deep that Formalism is still obscurely felt to be the spiritual property of Slavicists; perhaps the constructivistic approach of the Formalists is no longer seasonable in a country in which literary construction itself seems to have joined a long list of extinct or vanishing handicrafts and other skills. Yet Formalism yields insights which are structurally unique and unlike those afforded by the traditional "methods."

Let us choose, for a demonstration of the specificity of the Formalist procedure, Dante's *Paradiso*. The content of this poem may be taken as the ultimate which a writer has attempted to express, either as a vision of quintessential reality, or as a language which sets itself the task of fixing the inexpressible. Yet the events of *Paradiso* are, when juxtaposed with those of the other canticles, curiously self-referential. I do not only mean by that the absence in them of any genuine resistance or stubbornness in the matter itself —an absence which they share with other forms of science fiction, whether the sublime and theological, as in Milton or Wyndham Lewis, or the everyday interplanetary kind, and whose result is a kind of double pretense on the part of the writer that he is straining to render with precision a "world" which he has himself just finished inventing out of whole cloth.

In the earlier canticles the thoughts of Dante the character, his questions to Virgil and to the sinners, and their questions of him, just as frequently dealt with the reality of earth itself, and of individual destinies past and to come —a reality which lay outside or beyond the confines of the journey recounted. Now, however, the overwhelming preoccupation of the traveller is with the order of the realm before him and the nature of paradise itself: the content of *Paradiso* may therefore be said to be the order of an order. And even this order is itself but a figure or appearance:

> Qui se mostraron, non perchè sortita
> sia questa spera lor, ma per far segno
> de la celestïal c'ha men salita.[38]

What Dante sees and travels through is therefore but a kind of celestial projection, in the cartographical sense. The souls are themselves in reality all gathered together in the Empyrean, in an indistinguishable beatitude, which is thus articulated into hierarchy and gradations of the blessed as though to conform to the temporal and differentiating categories of Dante's earthly mind and experience; or, what amounts to the same thing, as though to make themselves accessible to Dante's narrative language as it moves in time.

In this context, therefore, the much-admired line of Piccarda Donati, "E'n la sua voluntate è nostra pace"[39] assumes a somewhat different significance. Ordinarily taken to ex-

[38] Dante Alighieri, *La Divina Commedia, Paradiso*, iv, vv. 37-39: "They are shown here, not because they have really emerged from their proper place [in the Empyrean], but to provide a visual embodiment of heaven's lowest circle."

[39] *Paradiso*, iii, v. 85.

86

press the abdication of the will and the release of the soul in submission, the verse forms part of an example of such submission and is intended to explain why the souls in the lower circles of paradise feel no longing to mount higher in the realms of the blessed. The famous verse is thus a way of motivating the diversity of *Paradiso*, of generating difference out of apparently identical raw material and of multiplicity out of the primal unity of beatitude.

On a theological level the problem to be solved is the reconciliation, in Christianity, of individualism and ultimate spiritual transfiguration in a situation in which other religions have foreseen a kind of dissolution of the soul into the divine substance or else a kind of beatific extinction. It would not be difficult to show how in one way or another every episode in *Paradiso*, every discussion, every encounter, every reaction—Charles Martel's account of the genetic diversity of mankind; the emblematic juxtaposition of St. Francis and St. Dominic; the long excursus on the relationship between Solomon's secular wisdom and that afforded by grace; the Eagle, through whose throat so many thousands speak with a single voice; the very justification for the creation of the angels themselves, as perhaps the purest example of God's almost gratuitous reproduction of his own substance—function in their divers ways as the ground and explanation of their own diversity.

In political terms the problem becomes that of the reestablishment of the Empire, as that order which will supercede the moral anarchy of nascent Italian capitalism and permit a harmonious exercise of humanity's varied talents within the unified figure of the state itself. It has often been pointed out how the *Commedia* becomes more and more explicitly political as it moves from *Inferno* to *Paradiso*.

Yet from the point of view of Formalism, all such apparent content, whether we choose to express it in theological or political terms, is itself but an optical illusion projected by the peculiar structural problems of the text itself as they find their ongoing resolution in its composition. The formal problem which Dante faces in *Paradiso* is in other words that of telling the story of the timeless in time, of recounting identity in the language of difference, of allowing unity to come to voice through multiplicity. The solution is just as unexpected. Even while Dante the character interrogates the order of paradise and attempts to understand how it can have gradations, Dante the poet continues his poem and carries it forward. We may therefore say that the content of *Paradiso* turns out to be a series of investigations of how paradise could have content; that the events of the poem are "nothing more" than a series of dramatizations of the pre-conditions necessary for such events to be conceivable in the first place. The subject of the poem is its own coming into being. Such a formula is no doubt implicit in the Formalist approach, even though it remained for their successors in French Structuralism to give it programmatic expression as such.[40]

There is, no doubt, something inherently and we may say structurally exasperating about such an analysis to the degree that it systematically refuses content, and indeed aims at translating all such proposed content back into projections of the form. Husserl's bracketting was an analogous suspension of common-sense experience, which sets in again with all its daily force and evidence after the parenthesis is closed. But the Formalists are reluctant to close it.

The implication is that a work only seems to have a ref-

[40] The reader may find it instructive to compare this pastiche of Formalist analysis with Philippe Sollers' Structuralist interpretation in "Dante et la traversée de l'écriture," *Logiques* (Paris, 1968), pp. 44-77.

erent, or to intend a determinate content. In reality it speaks only of its own coming into being, of its own construction, under the determinate circumstances or formal problems in the context of which that construction takes place. Such a point of view is to a certain degree, I believe, itself an optical illusion, projected by the Formalist procedures, and I will deal with this type of projection at greater length when we come to the analogous moment in Structuralism.

Yet I believe that there is a certain sense in which this is so, and in which all literary works, at the same time that they speak the language of reference, also emit a kind of lateral message about their own process of formation. The event of the reading, in other words, only partially obliterates that earlier event of the writing upon which, as in a palimpsest, it is superposed. Such is, I think, the social basis of Formalism as a method, insofar as the work is work solidified, the product the end-result of production.

4. At the same time, in Formalist practice the paradoxical reversal we have been describing results in a peculiar devaluation of its own starting point. Its premise had been that the literature of the "baring of the device," the literature which defamiliarized its own techniques, was, with a few exceptions such as *Tristram Shandy*, a peculiarly modern one which in this way radically distinguished itself from that older literature in which the devices were deliberately concealed. Yet it would now seem as though the "baring of the device" were characteristic of all literature, for now ultimately all literary structures may be understood as taking themselves for their own object, as being "about" literature itself. At this point, then, the specific and unique structure of literary modernism turns out to be no more than the basic structure of literature in general.

We may state this contradiction in another, more defini-

89

tive way by pointing out that the idea of *ostranenie* or de-familiarization is and must always be a polemic one: it depends on the negation of the existing habits of thought or perception and is to that degree bound to them and dependent on them as well. It is in other words not a coherent concept in its own right, but a transitional, self-abolishing one. This is as clear in Formalist criticism as anywhere else, where the force of the revelation depends on your having previously believed in "content," and is gauged against your implicit shock at seeing the philosophical or psychological implications of Gogol, or *Don Quixote* brutally discarded in favor of a purely artistic, artisanal model. This is indeed not true only of Formalism but of much of the theoretical apparatus of modernism in general: of a theory like Brecht's *Verfremdungseffekt*, for instance, which was addressed to a public unaccustomed to the garish stylizations of German expressionism. But for generations which have been raised on modernistic and stylized art and decoration and for whom such stylization needs no defense and seems utterly natural, an inner tension and dynamism seems to have gone out of the polemic.

The same contradiction pursues Shklovsky in his own personal literary production and is perhaps responsible for that peculiarly historical form of the Hegelian unhappy consciousness which has been his. For he took the "baring of the device" to be the specifically contemporary mode of defamiliarization and technical renewal in literature, thus absolutely identifying his own unique personal and historical situation with the new itself. But the "tragic sense of life" implicit in the Formalist idea of perpetual artistic change, of an artistic permanent revolution, demands a kind of consent to change and to the inevitable wearing out of once-new procedures: in short, to one's own death. The logical development would be the weariness of the public with the

kind of self-conscious art practiced by Shklovsky and motivated by his theories; yet the "baring of the device" is not
just one technique among others, which can be replaced,
but rather the coming to consciousness of art as defamiliarization in the first place. So if it goes, the entire theory goes
with it; and what gave itself as universal law proves with
the turning over of the calendar to have been nothing more
than the ideology of the day in disguise.

5

1. This is, however, not quite the end of the story. If the
distortions resulting from Shklovsky's artistic and personal
dilemma are removed from the basic force he set in motion,
then there results a purified model on the order of Saussurean linguistics. It was the merit and the genius of Yury Tynyanov to have made himself the theoretician of this most
lucid and mathematical reconstruction of the Formalist
position.

One is tempted to explain Tynyanov's success in the same
literary-historical terms in which we have accounted for
Shklovsky's failure: the literary form developed by Tynyanov as a way of renewing literature was not the peculiarly
contradictory and self-conscious "baring of the device" practiced by Shklovsky, but rather the selection of one technique from among others of equivalent functionality, of one
form among other equally privileged forms possible—namely the adventure novel, and in particular the historical adventure novel, as a genre never fully exploited in Russian
literature up to that time. Thus, by his practice of the form,
Tynyanov must have been able to see himself, not as fulfill-
ing literary history, but as taking part in but one moment of
a genuinely historical succession. The content of these
novels—most of them novelized biographies of writers from
the Pushkin period and of Pushkin himself—is moreover the

sign of a sensibility perhaps more historical in caste than the memorializing and autobiographical impulse that prevails in Shklovsky.

Tynyanov was able to preserve the idea of system in the analysis of the individual work of art by removing the notion of technique and the distortions implicit in the artisanal model which we have discussed above. The very teleological implications of the idea of technique lead to the false problem of the status of philosophical or other content in the work of art—that is to say, whether the latter exists "in order to" produce the former, or the former "in order to" produce the latter. If, however, one abandons the idea of technique and purpose, and speaks simply of dominant and secondary elements, or of a dominant constructional principle which is simply "the promotion of one group of factors at the expense of others"[41] (or of the "foregrounding" of one set of elements, a later but most expressive term developed by the Prague Circle),[42] then at once a model is constructed which has all the advantages of the older Shklovskian doctrine and none of its drawbacks.

The new model remains profoundly dialectical in the manner in which the foregrounded or dominant techniques are perceived in a tension with the secondary or backgrounded ones. But this new version of artistic perception as a deviation from a norm has the advantage of including the norm within the work of art itself as the older elements relegated to the background; thus the latter no longer spill outside the work and over into what are ultimately social problems, i.e., the dominant tastes, the dominant literary modes of a period. In this sense, the synchronic structure of the work

[41] Yury Tynyanov, *Problema stixotvornogo yazyka* (Leningrad, 1924), p. 10 (*Théorie de la littérature*, ed. Todorov, p. 118).
[42] See Paul Garvin, ed., *A Prague School Reader on Esthetics, Literary Structure, and Style* (Washington, D.C., 1955), esp. pp. 21-25.

includes diachrony in that it carries within itself as a negated or cancelled element those dominant modes of the immediately preceding generation against which it stands as a decisive break, and in terms of which its own novelties and innovations are understood.

2. Now for the first time this internal purity of the literary system permits the problem of the relationship to other nonliterary systems to be clearly posed. It will be that of elaborating some ultimate system of systems whose terms are not yet given (for dialectical thinking, this ultimate system of systems would be history itself, while for the Structuralists, as we will see shortly, it is language). This development, which has sometimes been described as the Formalists' attempt to conciliate Marxism, proves in reality to be but a logical consequence of their own thinking.

It is true that Tynyanov distinguishes between the evolution of a system according to its own inner laws and dynamism, and its forcible modification by the action on it of other systems from the outside; the historical and political reference is obvious. But what he is trying to describe are in reality two possible movements of relationship from one system to another: when the purely literary system, a kind of "imperialism striving towards the annexation of as large a territory as possible,"[43] absorbs elements of other systems into itself and uses them according to its own laws, then we may continue to speak of its autonomous evolution. When literature is absorbed into some other system, for whatever reason, then that evolution is bound to be suspended or even altered.

Tynyanov sees the various systems, at a given moment of history, as standing at relatively fixed distances from each

---

[43] Yury Tynyanov, *Arkhaisty i novatory* (Leningrad, 1929), p. 24 (*Die literarische Kunstmittel und die Evolution in der Literatur*, trans. A. Kaempfe [Frankfurt, 1967], p. 30).

other. Relationships between the most distant ones are therefore mediated by the intervening systems, particularly by
those standing closest to the literary system itself, namely
the system of "everyday life," and its own sub-systems of
verbal expression. Thus, for instance, a society in which
letter-writing is a particularly absorbing and intrinsically interesting activity offers a unique type of verbal raw material which under given circumstances was absorbed into
the literary system in the form of the letter-novel. Thus,
also, a society in which verbal eloquence and oratory were
widely practiced and valued and formed an integral, functional part of the socio-economic structure, as in the Arab
countries, as in Ireland (Joyce's *Ulysses!*), would offer a
type of verbal raw material, a pre-sketched ratio of poetry
to prose, a survival of tropes and rhetorical devices, not at
all analogous to the situation of the word in the mass-media
situation of the West. In this light we are able to reevaluate
Eichenbaum's discovery of Gogol's relationship to the *skaz*,
which becomes a privileged example of just such an annexation by art-prose of popular verbal elements surviving in the
culture.

The Formalists do not really seem to have been willing
to go much further towards a sociology of literature than
this. They tended to denounce as eclecticism more explicit
attempts to connect literature with the systems farthest away
from it, such as the economic.[44] They were, of course,
quite right to do so when the relationships and influences
claimed were formulated as immediate rather than mediated
and indirect: for their own system allowed for the latter,

[44] See in particular Eichenbaum's essay "V ozhidanii literatury," in
Literatura (*Teoria, Kritika, Polemika*), pp. 291-295 ("In Erwartung
der Literatur," in *Aufsätze zur Theorie und Geschichte der Literatur,*
trans. A. Kaempfe [Frankfurt, 1965], pp. 53-70).

and indeed in the long run that is the only allowance necessary to make a genuine literary sociology, a sociology of forms, possible.

3. The principal difference in emphasis between this Formalist model and a genuine theory of literary content such as that of Lukács lies in the degree to which the development of the work of art is seen to be influenced by the availability of the proper raw material. Tynyanov, as a practicing novelist, was well aware of this problem, as the following comments, implicitly directed against Shklovsky, show: "Let's take the possibility of a Russian adventure novel as an example. The principle of a novel with plot arises as a dialectical antithesis to the principle of the plotless novel. But the new constructional principle hasn't yet found adequate application, it must for the moment be content with foreign materials. In order to blend with Russian materials, certain pre-conditions must first be satisfied. This requirement is not so easy to meet. Subject meets style under conditions which no one knows until after it happens. If those conditions are lacking, the new phenomenon never gets beyond the trial stage."[45]

The insistence in this passage on the enabling role of the appropriate content or raw material, as well as on the ex post facto and non-predictive nature of literary analysis, is quite consistent with such sociological and Marxist analyses as those made by Lukács of the historical novel. There also, the development of the historical novel as a form is dependent on the adequate state and availability of its raw materials. In good Formalist fashion these raw materials are not simply knowledge of the past, availability of documents, local color, etc., but rather consciousness of the past and

[45] *Arkhaisty i novatory*, p. 19 (*Die literarische Kunstmittel*, pp. 23-24).

historical sensibility, which lies ready to hand in the time of Scott and has evolved into something more brittle and less serviceable in the time of Flaubert. An adequate picture of literary evolution, in its relationship to the other extra-literary systems, is, I think, possible on this condition: that content, available raw material, be seen, not as mere inert lumber, but as that which favors or impedes the development of the literary form which makes use of it. At that point, the closest extra-literary system in question can itself be interrogated on its relationship to its own neighboring systems. Thus, to return to our earlier example, the degree to which a given society has remained oral, has retained, for instance, oratorical usages and values, is itself a function of the economic and social development of the society and can be investigated accordingly.

4. What we have been describing so far is a relatively synchronic phenomenon, the relationship, in a given moment of time or history, of the literary system to neighboring and more distant ones in the totality of experience. The picture of actual literary history, actual change, remains problematical in Formalism. Even Tynyanov retains Saussure's basic model of change, in which the essential mechanisms at work are the ultimate abstractions of Identity and Difference. But where all history is understood as the operation of a single mechanism, it is transformed back into synchrony, and time itself becomes a kind of a-historical, relatively mechanical repetition.

Let Eichenbaum, the most pugnacious and combative of the group, once more be the spokesman for this anti-diachronic tendency of Formalism at its most extreme. The following passage looks ahead to Althusser at the same time that it signals the ultimate internal limitations of Formalist doctrine and method:

96

"The real Lermontov is the *historical* Lermontov. To avoid misunderstanding I must stipulate that I do not by this mean Lermontov considered as an individual event in *time*—an event which we would then be simply called on to restore. Time and the comprehension of the past which goes along with it does not constitute the basis for historical knowledge. Time in history is a fiction, a convention which plays an auxiliary role. We do not study movement in time; rather, movement as such is a *dynamic* process which can neither be subdivided in any way nor ever broken off, one which therefore has nothing to do with *real* time and cannot be measured in terms of it. The study of history reveals the dynamics of events, laws which function not only within the limits of some particular given period but everywhere and at all times. In this sense, as paradoxical as it may sound, history is the science of the permanent, the unchanging, the immobile, even where it deals with change and movement. It can be scientific only to the degree that it succeeds in transforming real movement into patterns or models [*chertyozh*]. Historical lyricism, the fondness for this or that period in and for itself, does not constitute science. To study a historical event does not in the least mean to describe it in isolation, as though it had meaning only in the setting of its own time. Such is the naive historicism which impedes scientific research. The real task is not some simple *projection into the past*, but rather that of understanding the historical *actuality* of an event, of determining its role in that development of historical energy which, in its very essence permanent, neither emerges nor disappears and for that very reason operates beyond time. *A fact historically understood is one which has been withdrawn from time* [italics mine]. In history there is never any repetition, simply because nothing ever disappears but only changes shape. For this reason,

97

historical analogies are not only possible but indispensable, and it is the study of historical events outside the dynamics of history, as unique and 'unrepeatable' ones, having their own isolated system, which is impossible, for it contradicts the very nature of such events."[46]

[46] Boris Eichenbaum, *Lermontov* (Leningrad, 1924), pp. 8-9 (*Aufsätze zur Theorie und Geschichte der Literatur*, pp. 102-103).

III

The Structuralist Projection

But what, then, is the meaning of these two words, "same" and "other"? Are they two new kinds other than the three [being, rest, and motion], and yet always of necessity intermingling with them, and are we to have five kinds instead of three; or when we speak of the same and other, are we unconsciously speaking of one of the first three kinds?   —Plato, *The Sophist*

FRENCH Structuralism is related to Russian Formalism, less as nephew to uncle, in Shklovsky's phrase, than as crossed cousins within an endogamous kinship system. Both ultimately derive from Saussure's foundational distinction between *langue* and *parole* (and, of course, from the distinction between synchrony and diachrony which lies behind it), but they exploit it in different ways. The Formalists were ultimately concerned with the way in which the individual work of art (or *parole*) was perceived differentially against the background of the literary system as a whole (or *langue*). The Structuralists, however, dissolving the individual unit back into the *langue* of which it is a partial articulation, set themselves the task of describing the organization of the total sign-system itself.

We may therefore understand the Structuralist enterprise as a study of superstructures, or, in a more limited way, of ideology. Its privileged object is thus seen as the unconscious value system or system of representations which orders social life at any of its levels, and against which the individual, conscious social acts and events take place and become comprehensible. Alternately, we may say that as a method, Structuralism may be considered one of the first consistent and self-conscious attempts to work out a philosophy of models (constructed on the analogy with language): the presupposition here is that all conscious thought takes place within the limits of a given model and is in that sense determined by it. It is only fair to add that for the most part these terms are not what the Structuralists themselves would have chosen to describe their work, so that what fol-

101

lows must in one way or another justify them, as a putting in perspective which is at the same time an implicit judgement.[1]

1

1. In particular the words "superstructure" and "ideology" suggest a deliberate juxtaposition of Structuralist research with the traditional Marxist problematics. But it is worth noting that where Saussure seems to have had no particular awareness of Marx at all, where for the Formalists Marxism, in its Soviet form, constituted little more than a source of polemics and an ideological adversary, the French Structuralists are on the contrary the beneficiaries of a Marxist culture, if only in the sense that they are no longer free to ignore the theoretical problems raised by the Marxist tradition: indeed, they know Marx so well as to seem constantly on the point of translating him into something else (the same is true of Freud, as we shall see later on).

Thus in spite of the unsystematic and even erratic character of many of Lévi-Strauss' theoretical asides, we must, I think, take him seriously when he declares that his work is designed "to contribute to that theory of superstructures which Marx barely sketched out."[2] It is certainly the case that for the most part Marxism itself has conceived of ideology only in the crudest fashion as a type of mystification or deliberate class distortion, and has failed to provide a really systematic exploration of superstructures. On the other hand, the constitutive feature of an apprehension of super-

---

[1] See for instance Althusser's attack on the concept of model (Louis Althusser, *Lire le Capital*, Vol. I [Paris, 1968], pp. 148-149); Lacan's attack on the notion of analogy (Jacques Lacan, *Écrits* [Paris, 1966], pp. 889-892); Barthes' distinction between semiological and ideological criticism (Roland Barthes, *Mythologies* [Paris, 1957], p. 245). It should be added that to anticipate possible philosophical objections to a given position—Lévi-Strauss and Foucault are particularly adept at this—is not necessarily the same as replying to them.

[2] Claude Lévi-Strauss, *La Pensée sauvage* (Paris, 1962), p. 173.

structures lies, as we have shown elsewhere,[3] in the mental operation by which the apparently independent ideological phenomenon is forcibly linked back up with the infrastructure: by which the false autonomy of the superstructure is dispelled, and with it that instinctive idealism which characterizes the mind when it has to do with nothing but spiritual facts. Thus the very concept of the superstructure is designed to warn us of the secondary character of the object which it names. The term is designed to point beyond its reference towards that which it is not, towards that material and economic situation which is its ultimate reality. It would seem, therefore, that one cannot place a superstructure between parentheses for descriptive and analytical purposes and still remain true to the impulse behind the terminology; this is so even if, as Lévi-Strauss feels, the forms of linguistic organization which he has revealed are those which characterize the superstructure as a whole. Now it is the form of research which remains idealistic, in that optical illusion of the autonomy of the sphere of superstructures which it encourages by the complete isolation of the latter from any consideration of the base.[4]

Lévi-Strauss has, however, an answer to this objection, in the form of a quotation from Engels himself: "To work out

superstructure

[3] In my *Marxism and Form*, esp. pp. 4-5.

[4] Compare the following observation of Marx on Proudhon: "The only trouble with this method is that when he begins the analysis of one of these phases, M. Proudhon cannot explain it without referring to all the other social relationships, relationships which he has however not yet engendered by the movement of his dialectic. When he then, through the use of pure reason, passes along to the birth of the other phases, he acts as though they were new-born children, he forgets that they have the same age as the first. . . . When one uses the categories of political economy to construct the edifice of an ideological system, one disjoins the members of the social system. One changes the different parts of society into so many separate self-contained societies which succeed each other." (*Misère de la philosophie*, quoted in Althusser, *Lire le Capital*, Vol. I, p. 121.)

this parallel between the Germans of Tacitus and the American redskins, I made modest extracts from the first volume of your Bancroft. The resemblance is all the more striking in that the mode of production is so utterly different—here a hunting and fishing culture without stock-breeding or agriculture, there nomadic pastoralism passing into field cultivation. Which shows precisely just how much less decisive the mode of production is at this stage than the relative breakdown of the older kinship system and of the tribe's initial distribution of women. . . ."[5] Thus Lévi-Strauss' method would seem to be justified by the peculiarity of his privileged object of study, for in a sense the groups whose superstructures he examines do not really possess an infrastructure in the sense of modern economics. At the very least, it would seem that in societies in which the division between material production and other activities has not yet taken place, the very notion of a separate superstructure becomes problematical. And so does that of an infrastructure as well: how ultimately is one to distinguish between the material and spiritual dimensions of a technique of planting which is at one and the same time a religious ritual?

What has happened here is that Structuralism has tended to replace the older mind/body opposition which continues to inform the classical distinction between superstructure and infrastructure (the one involving material goods and physical need, the other mental operations and cultural products) with a new kind. We have tried to show how the Saussurean revolution corresponded to a historic shift in the subject-matter of the sciences in general, where the visible, physical independence of a given object (the organism of animals, the characteristics of chemical elements) no longer seems a useful way of distinguishing the appropriate

[5] In a letter to Marx, 8 December 1882, quoted in Lévi-Strauss, *Anthropologie structurale* (Paris, 1958), p. 372.

units of study; where the first task of a science henceforth seems the establishment of a method, or a model, such that the basic conceptual units are given from the outset and organize the data (the atom, the phoneme). This gradual shift in the sciences from perception to models corresponds to a transformation of social life itself, where with the monopolistic period of capitalism, the distinction between primary and secondary industry, becomes blurred, as does that between products that satisfy genuine needs and luxury items whose consumption is henceforth stimulated artificially by advertising.

At this point, therefore, the mind/body opposition is transformed into a structural or conceptual distinction between significance on the one hand, and the meaningless physical substratum or *hylé* by which that significance is invested. Henceforth, what was an external line of cleavage, in that it separated spiritual or cultural phenomena from material ones, becomes an internal distinction, implying that every phenomenon carries within itself both superstructure and infrastructure, both culture and nature, both meaning and raw material. At this point, then, the problem of superstructures becomes, if anything, more complex than Lévi-Strauss suggests.

2. Yet there is another sense in which Structuralism finds itself condemned to the study of ideology, not by choice, but out of a kind of internal necessity. For the principal conceptual instrument of Saussurean linguistics was, as we recall, the sign, the originality of which was to have distinguished not two, but three, elements in the process of speech: not only the word and its referent in the real world, but also, within the individual word or sign, a relationship between the signifier (or acoustic image) and the signified (or concept). The emphasis on this relationship tended, as we have shown, to exclude any consideration of the thing

105

itself, of the object of reference in the "real world." This declaration of independence of linguistics from any purely semantic concerns we compared to Husserl's technique of bracketting in phenomenology. It was this linguistic "epoche" also which enabled the Russian Formalists to operate their critical revolution as well, reversing the priorities such that henceforth everything—meaning, world view, the author's life—exists in order to permit the work itself to come into being.

In the framework of the Structuralist enterprise this principle has the effect of reinforcing idealistic tendencies which are already at work within the material itself, of encouraging the insulation of the superstructure from reality. This is not merely an external judgment, but a contradiction within Structuralism as well: for its concept of the sign forbids any research into the reality beyond it, at the same time that it keeps alive the notion of such a reality by considering the signified as a concept *of* something.

The writer who has dealt the most consequentially with this dilemma is one who approaches it, paradoxically, from the standpoint of orthodox dialectical materialism, and whose work may therefore be taken as a kind of reconciliation between the Lenin of *Materialism and Empiriocriticism* and the Saussurean heritage. The originality of Althusser is to have reversed the terms of the older materialistic epistemology, for which reality is "outside the mind" and truth a kind of adequation with reality which it would seem rather difficult to verify. For Althusser, in a sense, we never really get outside our own minds: both ideology and genuine philosophical investigation, or what he calls "theoretical praxis," run their course in the sealed chamber of the mind; materialism is thus preserved by an insistence on the essentially idealistic character of all thinking. Indeed, it would seem that on one level ideology is distinguished from theory in that the latter recognizes its own idealistic (or simply ideational) character while the former attempts to pass itself off as reality. On another level, ideology would seem to be that grillwork of form, convention, and belief which orders our actions, and theory the quite different conscious production of knowledge. Thus, even in a socialist society ideology will retain a function.[6]

There are therefore two types of concrete phenomena: concrete reality and concrete thought. "The process which produces a concrete object on the level of knowledge takes place entirely within the realm of theoretical practice: it has to do, of course, with the concrete object on the level of reality, but this concrete reality 'subsists after as before in its independence, on the outside of the mind' (Marx), without ever being able to be assimilated to that other type of 'concrete object' which is knowledge of it."[7] Thus, if properly seized, theory is also a kind of production: it works with tangible objects which have already been produced (the earlier theories or concrete thoughts) and transforms them into new objects, as in the production of the material world. Althusser's object of study is primarily the history of science (including Marx's discoveries), and within such limits, it is not difficult to see why he understands the production of knowledge as being essentially work on a preexisting idea: the latter, ideology or inadequate conceptualization (he calls it Generality I), is transformed into precise scientific knowledge (Generality III), by the operation of theoretical

[6] See in particular Louis Althusser, *Pour Marx* (Paris, 1965), pp. 238-243. "It is clear that *ideology* (*as a system of mass representations*) *is indispensable in any society in order to form men, to transform them and to make them able to respond to the requirements of their living conditions.* . . . It is in ideology that the classless society *lives* the inadequation-adequation of its relationship to the world, in and through ideology that it transforms the 'consciousness' of men, which is to say their attitudes and actions, in order to make them equal to their tasks and their living conditions" (p. 242).

[7] *Ibid.*, pp. 189-190.

107

praxis (Generality II). (We will see later on what this scheme of knowing as the preparation of a product which is the "concrete-in-thought" becomes when the *Tel Quel* group transfers it to the area of literary creation or the "production of the text.")

If we ask what relationship can be established between the sphere of purely ideational production and that of material reality, then it would seem that Althusser has two kinds of solutions: one on the side of the object of thought, the other on the side of the thinker. The first, which we will deal with later in more detail, reveals an intermediary object between thought and reality, and that is the "problématique," or hierarchical structure of problems, and which transmits the shifts in external, historical reality to the theoretician at work within the mind, for it is nothing more or less than "the objective problems posed for ideology by the historical moment itself."[8] From the point of view of the thinker, however, only the distinction between a theoretical and a political praxis would seem to provide the possibility for acting on a real, even though indirectly knowable, world. Umberto Eco has suggested that Althusser's ultimate point of reference in this dilemma is Spinoza himself: "Marxist philosophy would thus be able to act on the world because —ultimately—*ordo et connexio idearum idem est ac ordo et connexio rerum.*"[9] In any case, since for Althusser real historical time is only indirectly accessible to us, action for him would seem to be a kind of blindfolded operation, a manipulation at distance, in which we could at best watch our own performance indirectly, as though in a mirror, reading it back from the various readjustments of consciousness which result from the alteration in the external situation itself.

Whatever the merits of this intricate solution, the basic

[8] *Ibid.*, p. 64, n. 30.
[9] Umberto Eco, *La Struttura assente* (Milan, 1968), p. 360, n. 192.

108

terms of the problem have now become recognizable: it is essentially a replay of the Kantian dilemma of the unknowability of the thing-in-itself. Lévi-Strauss, in discussing the nature of superstructure, deliberately adopts a Kantian terminology: "We believe that between *praxis* and custom [*pratiques*] a mediator is always interposed which is the conceptual schema through whose operation a matter and a form both of which lack independent existence are able to come into being as structures. . . . The dialectic of superstructures, like that of language, consists in postulating *constitutive unities*, which can only play this role if they are defined unequivocally, that is to say by contrasting them by pairs, in order by means of such constitutive unities to elaborate a *system* which will finally play the role of a synthetic operator between the idea and the fact, transforming this last into a *sign*."[10]

Thus, as in Kant also, the separation of these mental processes from reality encourages an explicit search for the permanent structures of the mind itself, the organizational categories and forms through which the mind is able to experience the world, or to organize a meaning in what is essentially in itself meaningless. It is not enough to dismiss this dilemma on the grounds that for Structuralism there is no thing-in-itself, only the articulations of language according to its various structures: this position merely displaces the problem from Kant to his successors in German objective idealism without solving it. In any case, in practice, all the Structuralists: Lévi-Strauss with his idea of nature, Barthes with his feeling for social and ideological materials, Althusser with his sense of history, *do* tend to presuppose, beyond the sign-system itself, some kind of ultimate reality which,

[10] *La Pensèe sauvage*, pp. 173-174. And see his enthusiastic endorsement of the aims of a Kantian critical philosophy in *Le Cru et le cuit* (Paris, 1964), pp. 18-20.

unknowable or not, serves as its most distant object of reference.

There are, no doubt, other possible solutions implicit in the initial terms of Structuralism itself: according to one, the ontire sign-system would somehow correspond to all of reality, without there being any one-to-one correspondance in the individual elements at any point. From another, more positivistic point of view which is that of Lévi-Strauss, as well as in the Spinozistic solution ascribed above to Althusser, there would be some "pre-established harmony" between the structures of the mind (and ultimately of the brain) and the order of the outside world. For the moment, however, it is enough for us to indicate this epistemological dilemma as the outer limit or boundary of the Structuralist framework, one to which we will return at the end of this essay.

3. On entering the area of concrete Structuralist research itself, however, we may continue to use the idea of the sign, with its various articulations, as a kind of exploratory map. Indeed, Barthes has already made an initial classification, on its basis, of the three basic varieties of Structuralism or what we might call the three main styles of semiology: the symbolic, primarily sensitive to the relationship between signifier and signified; the paradigmatic, chiefly apprehending the resemblance of whole classes of signs among each other; and the syntagmatic, which works primarily with the interaction between a given sign and its context, between signs among themselves (and these last two groups correspond respectively to the metaphoric and metonymic feeling for signs).[11] But this classification is a relatively internal one for our purposes, and perhaps one still too involved with the claims of semiology for itself.

[11] See "L'Imagination du signe," in Barthes, *Essais critiques* (Paris, 1964).

In any case, we have preferred a cruder classification for the purposes of the presentation that follows, where, following the internal structure of the sign itself, we will distinguish those investigations that aim primarily at the organization of the signifier; those which take as their object the signified; and, finally, those which attempt to isolate the process of signification itself, the very emergence of an initial relationship between signifier and signified.

2

> Only the relationship of one signifier to another signifier engenders the relationship of signifier to signified.
>
> —Lacan[12]

1. The originality of Structuralism lies in its insistence on the signifier. It involves a preliminary operation which isolated the signifier as such, as an object of study, from what it signified. For the essential place of structure is that of the organization of signifiers among themselves. And it is here also that the problem of the scope of semiology as a science arises: whether, as Saussure thought, linguistics is to be seen as simply a branch of some vaster science of signs and sign-systems, or whether, as Barthes has come to believe,[13] semiology is itself simply to be considered a branch of linguistics. As is well known, the privileged objects of Structuralist investigation are very often non-verbal sign-systems: the most famous being Lévi-Strauss' theory of kinship for which "marriage rules and the systems of kinship [are] considered a kind of language, that is to say, a set of operations designed to ensure a certain type of communication between individuals and groups. That the 'message' is here made up of the *women of the group* who *circulate*

---

[12] Quoted in A. G. Wilden, *The Language of the Self* (Baltimore, Maryland, 1968), p. 239.

[13] See "Eléments de sémiologie," in Roland Barthes, *Le degré zéro de l'écriture* (Paris, 1964), p. 81.

111

Levi Strauss—
totemism
is a kind
of language

between the clans, dynasties or families (and not as in language itself by the *words of the group* circulating between individuals) does not affect the basic identity of the phenomenon in both cases."[14] Thus, in this example of a non-linguistic sign-system, the priority of the language model is maintained; and even in more distant phenomena, such as Barthes' intricate anatomy of clothing styles, or Lévi-Strauss' "culinary triangle," in which the styles of the various cuisines are analyzed into a series of oppositions between the cooked, the raw, and the rotten (a triad which can itself be recombined into various possible dualisms), the priority of language, either as a model or as a mediator, seems to hold good. We will confront this problem again when we deal with the dimension of the signified as such; for the moment, it suffices to evoke Barthes' hesitation: "Does there exist any system of objects of any dimension that can do without articulated language? Is not the word the fatal relay of any signifying order?"[15]

We will therefore confine our illustrations here to sign-systems which are already inherently verbal, namely to myth and literature. At this point, however, it is necessary to recall a methodological opposition which has its origin in Saussure himself, and which results in two types, or rather two levels, of possible linguistic analysis: the one phonological, at work within the word itself, and operating with the tiniest units of intelligible organization, the phonemes, themselves unintelligible when taken separately; the other that of syntagmatic and paradigmatic analysis at work on the level of the sentence itself, or combination of signs.

2. Lévi-Strauss' analysis of myth in particular seems to take place on what we might call the phonological or microscopic level: for the myth is according to him not so much

---

[14] *Anthropologie structurale*, p. 69.
[15] Roland Barthes, *Système de la mode* (Paris, 1967), p. 9.

a sentence as a single sign.[16] The various elements of the myth, therefore—the sorcerer, the jaguar, the snake, the hut, the wife, the herb, and so forth—are not in themselves meaningful entities, not so much comparable to individual words, as to individual phonemes. They have no intrinsic value in themselves, and Lévi-Strauss is at one with Propp in feeling that any classificatory system based on these elements of myth is a hopeless and misleading enterprise. But Propp, working within his own cultural materials, was in a sense able to disengage a basic equation or structure without having to work his way down to the basic mechanisms of mythological thought itself: which are essentially, for Lévi-Strauss, as in phonology, binary oppositions.

The binary opposition is therefore at the outset a heuristic principle, that instrument of analysis on which the mythological hermeneutic is founded. We would ourselves be tempted to describe it as a technique for stimulating perception, when faced with a mass of apparently homogeneous data to which the mind and the eyes are numb: a way of forcing ourselves to perceive difference and identity in a wholly new language the very sounds of which we cannot yet distinguish from each other. It is a decoding or deciphering device, or alternately, a technique of language learning. At the same time this method presupposes a vast body of raw material or data, following the basic principle of communication theory that the communicational success of a message is in direct proportion to the amount of redundancy it contains. Thus Lévi-Strauss, in his analyses, will include all available versions of a given myth, without attempting to determine historical priority or authenticity of one of them over the others.

The series *Mythologiques* offers a vast repertoire of In-

---

[16] Lévi-Strauss and Roman Jakobson have called their detailed analyses of poems by Baudelaire "microscopies."

113

dian myths of the two Americas. But what Lévi-Strauss aims at here is not so much the analysis of any particular individual myth as it is the mechanisms of transformation by which the mythical structure is recombined or articulated into its various utterances or versions, which thus ultimately form a whole constellation of related structures, much like the sub-species of the biological kingdom. No doubt this dissolution of the individual *parole*, this emphasis on the system itself, is implicit in Structuralism from the outset.

Here also we may best grasp the analogies between Lévi-Strauss' interpretive techniques and those of Freud in *The Interpretation of Dreams*. Both are profoundly contextual in the manner in which they go about deciphering the individual elements of their respective "texts." For Freud the dream is a *parole* which can be understood only against the background of that unique and private *langue* which is the dreamer's past and present, the events of his personal history and chance associations of his life experience. In much the same way, for Lévi-Strauss the value of a given element of a myth is forever bound to the unique social and geographical experience of the tribe in question, to its taxonomic codes, the accidents of its history—insofar as the latter can be known—climate, social organization, and so forth. For both modes of interpretation, therefore, the "symbol" is a profoundly arbitrary sign—an image which would be readily comprehensible had it remained within the initial tissue of reasoning and abstract conjecture that produced it, but which now, as a kind of shorthand, has been shorn of the latter and left to stand by itself. Thus under certain conditions the jaguar may be understood to express the theme of fire, and indeed to embody the very origins of fire: for the jaguar eats meat, and since meat cannot be eaten without being cooked, it is felt that he must necessarily know the secret of fire. At the same time, it is clear that whereas men now have fire, the jaguar no longer does: thus an explanation (in narrative form) must be evolved to account for the fact that the jaguar, even while conferring fire on men, lost it himself.[17] The image of the jaguar is thus a schematic representation of this whole buried or unconscious syllogistic train of thought; and the example may also serve to convey the difficulty of any direct and immediate application of either of these two contextual hermeneutics to the interpretation of literature itself, in which an external context (supplied by patient or by native informant) is not available in the same way.

When we turn now from such an investigation of the raw material or associative clusters of mythology to the analysis of a single myth, we find the binary opposition at work in a more strict formal way, both as underlying structure and as a method of revealing that structure. In his henceforth classic analysis of the Oedipus myth,[18] Lévi-Strauss begins by sorting the constitutive elements into distinctive combinations of opposites. Alongside examples of an "overestimation of the kinship bond"—not only incest, but Antigone's unlawful protection of her dead brother's body as well—there come to be ranged episodes which reflect what might be called an "underestimation" of the same relationships: the murder of the father, the struggle between the brothers, and so forth. These two groups, therefore, make up an initial binary opposition; and we should point out here that it is precisely the concept of an organization by oppositions which permits us to verify experimentally the categories or groupings of the episodes. If the latter are arbitrarily chosen —as would be, for instance, in this case a group based on the notion of a burial or a burying—then they will not find

[17] *Le Cru et le cuit*, p. 91.
[18] In "La Structure des mythes," *Anthropologie structurale*, esp. pp. 235-240.

any oppositions in the series. There is therefore at work here a profoundly relational type of thinking, in which it is the initial opposition or difference which founds the category of the class, rather than—as in ordinary classification —the resemblance or identity of two or more elements which suggests the existence of a category.

In the Oedipus myth, the pair of oppositions described above is itself opposed to another pair of oppositions, whose elaboration is even more revealing. For through the latter we attempt to sort out various other random elements of the myth, among them Oedipus' name (swollen foot) and the analogous names of his forefathers, the sphinx, Cadmus' dragon, and so forth. I give the solution at once, before commenting on the process: in these elements we are to see an opposition between a human victory over the monstrous (Cadmus' slaying of the dragon, Oedipus' triumph over the sphinx), and a state of physical deformity in which the human being remains partially under the power of the monstrous. We may roughly describe this opposition as one between autochthony, the origination of man from the earth, his subservience to nature, and his liberation from the earth or natural forces. In terms of the themes of kinship, therefore, the myth would essentially dramatize the difference between two concepts of man's origination: the one on the vegetal mode, an emergence of man from earth or his autochthony; the other his birth from the union of human parents, a concept which essentially serves to negate that of autochthony. What I wish to stress here is that this working out or arrangement into an opposition (I will not yet call it an interpretation) does not take place with anywhere near the same ease as the first grouping, whose content (the family relationships) seemed to dictate itself. Here we seem to work our way up from the concrete details through the

116

various levels of generalization, until we reach a degree of abstraction sufficient to permit the concept of the Monstrous on the one hand to be assimilated to that of the Deformed on the other, both ultimately being subsumed under the generic idea of the Unnatural. Here, perhaps, we can witness at its clearest the process by which the idea of binary opposition generates an order out of random data, by that movement of ever more generalizing enlargements which we have described.

The meaning of the myth is located at the point of intersection between the two pairs of oppositions, of that opposition to the second power between them which Lévi-Strauss will henceforth call a contradiction. We will, however, postpone our treatment of that meaning, which is the moment of the actual interpretation of the myth, until later on in this chapter. For the moment, it is enough to underline the way in which the conceptual or heuristic instruments of the *mythologue* himself are assimilated to those of the original mythological thought. In and through such oppositions (which were his way of disengaging the structure of the myth) Lévi-Strauss sees a type of pre-scientific meditation on the part of the primitive myth-maker, a meditation on the more general categories involved, on the kinship relation, on nature, on generation out of the earth. The myth is one of the ways in which primitive man thinks about such problems: and in it the conceptual level (the categories which preside over the oppositions) and the perceptual or concrete are united in a kind of hieroglyphic or rebus-like language comparable, in the experience of civilized man, to dreams or to the fantasies of children.

Myths are therefore for Lévi-Strauss in one sense quite the opposite of real narration. This comes out perhaps the most clearly when the degraded myth passes over into an

117

anecdotal form which he compares to a kind of chronicle or primitive novel.[19] In these forms, instead of abolishing time and instituting the discontinuous, instead of using lived experience as little more than a storehouse of available symbolic elements for the construction of a code, the myth turns into an evocation of time and of continuity; from a structure, it becomes rather a search for structure (meaning) on the part of the hero, and the novel form comes into being, for which "the hero of the novel is the novel itself."

In its original state, however, the myth did not so much narrate (or constitute a sentence) as it did convey a message or value-system (and function as a single sign). Thus the myth, as an elaborate organization of latent conceptual categories, finds its ultimate fulfillment, not in the narratives of more sophisticated and historical (or temporally conscious) societies, but rather in that primitive form of science which Lévi-Strauss has described under the term of "pensée sauvage" (the play on the word "pensée" designates both the wild flower and thought growing wild in its natural environment) and which consists essentially in classification systems distinguished from our own in that they are based on physical perception and primary qualities rather than on the measurable and conceptual ones of Western science.

The evolution of this primitive science can be measured by the very structures of mounting generalization within the myth itself: "In order to construct this system of myths about cooking, we found ourselves obliged to use oppositions between terms all more or less drawn from sensory qualities: raw and cooked, fresh and rotten, and so forth. Now we find that the second step in our analysis reveals terms still opposed in pairs, but whose nature is different to the degree that they involve not so much a logic of quali-

---

[19] *L'Origine des manières de table*, pp. 104-106; and see above pp. 71-72.

ties as one of forms: empty and full, container and contents, internal and external, included and excluded, etc." Myth is therefore essentially an epistemological, rather than an existential, affair; its analysis shows that "the differential gaps exploited by myths lie not so much in the things themselves as in a body of common properties, expressible in geometric terms and all transformable into each other by means of operations which are already an algebra." Mythical thought is therefore a kind of philosophizing which is not yet aware of itself; or, conversely, we may see in the very birth of philosophy itself, in ancient Greece, "a moment in which mythical thought transcends itself and contemplates, beyond images still adhering to concrete experience, a world of concepts freed from this slavery, their relationships now freely defining themselves."[20]

One is tempted to wonder whether this logic is latent in the mind of primitive man himself, or simply in that of the *mythologue*, who finds his own operational categories returning back against him in tangible, sensory form. For the moment, however, we may limit our remarks to the concept of the binary opposition itself. It would not perhaps be too farfetched to see in it a kind of arrested dialectic, the projection of a multi-dimensional concept into a world of plane surfaces. The binary opposition is dialectical insofar as it is dynamic, insofar as it involves differential perception: it becomes analytic only when it hardens into a static, rather positivistic element of all structure, which then becomes an additive affair, a counting up of various oppositions. We may say all this another way by observing that both poles of the binary opposition are positive, both are existants, equally present to the naked eye: whereas what makes up a genuine dialectical opposition is that one of the

[20] Lévi-Strauss, *Du miel aux cendres* (Paris, 1966), pp. 406-408.

terms is negative, one is an absence. Thus Lévi-Strauss approaches a genuinely dialectical idea when he compares myth, as an existant, with narrative such as the novel, which defines the former in that it is that which myth is not. One of the terms of the dialectical opposition is always outside the work; it is the work's other side, its surface, or otherness, in the face of history itself. This movement, which transcends the individual phenomenon in question, is at one with the self-consciousness of dialectical thinking, quite different from the fashion in which objective scientific thought tends to hypostasize its objects. Lévi-Strauss' nostalgia for primitive culture and for myth is in this sense merely the formal distortion projected by his method; and I should add that Soviet semiology, which explicitly assimilates the binary opposition to a dialectic of presence and absence, does not give rise to the same contradictions.

3. We emerge from the microscopic analysis of the sign-system, from the structure of binary oppositions, into that of its larger syntax. The problem here is the invention of a single set of terms or elements (such as the binary opposition) into which the various empirical categories of syntax may be translated. The initial equivalence between the sign-statement on whatever level and the figures of language is unproblematical in itself. The following assimilation by Jacques Lacan of Freudian to rhetorical categories may serve as an ample illustration of the process:

"Take up the work of Freud again at the *Traumdeutung* to remind yourself that the dream has the structure of a sentence or, rather, to stick to the letter of the work, of a rebus; that is to say, it has the structure of a form of writing, of which the child's dream represents the primordial ideography and which, in the adult, reproduces the simultaneously phonetic and symbolic use of signifying elements, which can also be found both in the hieroglyphs of ancient Egypt and in the characters still used in China.

"But even this is no more than the deciphering of the instrument. The important part begins with the translation of the text, the important part which Freud tells us is given in the [verbal] elaboration of the dream—in other words, in its rhetoric. Ellipsis and pleonasm, hyperbaton or syllepsis, regression, repetition, apposition—these are the syntactical displacements; metaphor, catachresis, antonomasia, allegory, metonymy, and synechdoche—these are the semantic condensations in which Freud teaches us to read the intentions —ostentatious or demonstrative, dissimulating or persuasive, retaliatory or seductive—out of which the subject modulates his oneiric discourse."[21]

(Such linguistic investment of the Freudian dream work then returns with redoubled force in Althusser's application of it to historical events themselves, which are seen as causally *overdetermined* in the Freudian sense, forming processes of *displacement*—in the shift from one structure to another—and *condensation*—when in the revolutionary moment all the hitherto separate parts of the historical structure become profoundly politicized and identified with each other—and where political revolution itself is seen as something like the *Darstellung* or representation of those deeper contradictions in the infrastructure which thus ultimately "express themselves.")

Yet such an equivalence, which makes Freudian doctrine available as a hermeneutic, at this stage offers little more than the possibility of translation: an empirical classification of a given non-verbal signifier in one or the other rhetorical category. The assimilation is not really useful until all of the various linguistic or rhetorical devices can be

[21] Translated in Wilden, *The Language of the Self*, pp. 30-31.

121

shown to be derivations of a single function, and Lacan finds this unification in Roman Jakobson's influential theory of the opposition of metaphor to metonymy,[22] which designates a kind of global opposition between the synchronic mode (superposition, coexistence, the paradigmatic) and the diachronic (succession, the syntagmatic). Lacanian analysis attempts to translate psychic functions into these two ultimate linguistic operations, seeing in metaphor the origin of the symptom (in that it replaces one signifier with another), and in metonymy the origin of desire ("it is the connection of signifier to signifier which permits the elision through which the signifier installs the lack of being in the object relation, by using the power of 'reference back' of signification in order to invest it with the desire aimed at this lack which it supports").[23]

Even this ultimate opposition, however, becomes an empirical and merely classificatory affair unless it is itself subsumed under some single more dominant function (unless, in other words, it is shown precisely why all figures should be exhausted by these two primordial ones). I would suggest that its unity be found in the common situation of each figure with respect to speech itself, and in particular with respect to the incommensurability of language, the fact that language can never really express any *thing*: only relationships (Saussurean linguistics) or sheer absence (Mallarmé). Thus language has of necessity recourse to indirection, to substitution: itself a substitute, it must replace that empty center of content with something else, and it does so either by saying what the content is *like* (metaphor), or describing its context and the contours of its absence, listing the things

[22] See in particular "Two Aspects of Language and Two Types of Aphasic Disturbances," in Roman Jakobson and Morris Halle, *Fundamentals of Language* (The Hague, 1956), pp. 55-82.
[23] *The Language of the Self*, p. 114.

that border around it (metonymy). Thus language, by its very nature, is either analogical or fetishistic; in Frazer's terminology (describing the same general opposition in the forms of primitive magic) its operation is either homeopathic or contagious.[24] This resolution of the figures themselves back into their initial situation is quite consistent with the Lacanian doctrine of the primal lack, and suggests unexpected ways of dealing with old dilemmas. So, for instance, the vexed question of the relationship between traditional and modern literary methods, renewed only recently with Picard's attack on Barthes,[25] may be accounted for by the hypothesis that an intrinsic literary criticism is metaphorical, in that it seeks to replace the work with a description of its structures, with a new "metalanguage" which resembles it; while the older literary history, evoking as it did the furniture, the influences, and the historical period which surrounded the absent moment of creation, derived essentially from metonymy in its effort to conjure that absence into a momentary glimpse of the thing itself.

In the long run, however, the concepts of metaphor and metonymy cannot be isolated from each other and undergo a ceaseless metamorphosis from the one into the other before our very eyes. As a kind of ultimate binary opposition, they are really little more than a hypostasis of that basic dialectic of Identity and Difference with which Saussurean linguistics began.

4. The most fully developed syntactical analysis of the organization of the signifier is that which has been conducted in the name of a "grammar of plot" by A. J. Greimas along

[24] Sir James Frazer, *The Golden Bough* (one-volume abridged edition, New York, 1951), pp. 12-14.

[25] The principal exhibits in this dispute, which arose on the occasion of Barthes' rather Freudian *Sur Racine* (Paris, 1963), are Raymond Picard, *Nouvelle critique ou nouvelle imposture?* (Paris, 1965) and Roland Barthes, *Critique et vérité* (Paris, 1966).

with such critics as Barthes, Claude Bremond, and Tzvetan Todorov. This analysis, roughly analogous to Chomsky's generational grammar, prescribes a reduction of the various more superficial narrative levels of the text to a deeper structure which Greimas has called the "actantial model." The latter is, as Greimas has reminded us, essentially an "extrapolation of the structure of syntax,"[26] and may be said to involve the double metaphor of a grammar in which the older categories (subject, verb, object) reenact some primal dramatic representation upon the stage of the most varied types of discourse: "If we recall that *functions*, in traditional syntax, are but roles played by words—the subject being 'the one who performs the action,' the object 'the one who suffers it,' etc.—then according to such a conception the proposition as a whole becomes a spectacle to which *homo loquens* treats himself."[27] For Greimas, it is this underlying "dramatic" structure which is common to all forms of discourse, philosophical or literary, expository or affective alike: "This spectacle is however unique in that it is permanent: the content of the actions changes all the time, the actors vary, but the enunciation-spectacle remains forever the same, for its permanence is guaranteed by the fixed distribution of the basic roles."[28]

It is in order to distinguish between the surface content of the enunciation-spectacle (which may involve philosophical concepts or abstract entities just as much as the characters of ordinary narration) and this deeper underlying structure that Greimas evolves the term *actant*, which can be articulated either as a function (as the possibility of a certain type of performance) or as a qualification (involving the conferal of a certain number of attributes). Such a distinction permits us at once to reorganize our reading

[26] A. J. Greimas, *Sémantique structurale* (Paris, 1966), p. 185.
[27] *Ibid.*, p. 173.   [28] *Ibid.*

124

of a given text and to recognize more fundamental mechanisms at work beneath the surface. So, for instance, it may turn out that a character or actor in a given narrative in reality serves as a cover for two separate and relatively independent *actants*; or that two actors, independent personalities and separate characters in the story-line, amount to little more than alternating articulations of an *actant* structurally identical in both contexts.

Greimas has provisionally classed the possible uses of the *actant* as follows: as subject or object, in which form the basic event of the enunciation-spectacle will be that of a desire for an object; or as destinator or destinatee, in which case the basic event will take the form of a communication; or, finally, as auxiliary or adversary (*adjuvant* or *opposant*) in the action. These two final categories may be thought of as modal or auxiliary ones which play a syntactical role very much like such expressions as "with the greatest of difficulty" or "effortlessly" in the context of the individual sentence.

It seems more revealing in this connection to use the language of process rather than that of substance and to speak of the "actantial reduction" as a type of operation performed upon a text, instead of the "actantial model" as a static vision of structure. Such reduction borrows from linguistics its basic technique of commutation or systematic variation, according to which the analyst methodically substitutes alternate possibilities for the elements given in the text until he is able to reach that final set of functions which resists variation. Thus for the narrative specificity of the surface level, where the victim is strangled with his own necktie, we may substitute a series of variations (hanging, stabbing, or shooting), which themselves constitute in their turn specifications of the more basic category of injury (e.g., imprison, despoil, kill, rape). Todorov has in particular made a sug-

125

gestive inventory of the ways in which the narrative surface may frequently be said to constitute a kind of mood, in the grammatical sense, of some fundamental verbal function. Thus, in the *Decameron*, the love-passion may be seen as the optative of sexual intercourse, while renunciation may be thought of as its negative optative; the conditional frequently takes the form of the tasks familiar in fairy-tale or medieval romance; while the subjunctive of injury might be expressed as a simple threat; and so forth.[29]

We must here underscore a tendency which we found at work in an analogous moment of Formalism as well and which we must understand as a deformation structurally inherent in the method. This is the transformation of diachronic events into synchronic categories, the replacement of the event by the static concept, of the verb by the neologism. Greimas has himself evoked this tendency, as a kind of baleful spell hanging over linguistic analysis, "which, whenever one opens one's mouth to speak of relationships, causes the latter to be at once transformed, as though by enchantment, into substantives, or in other words into terms whose meaning we must then negate by postulating new relationships, and so forth. Any metalanguage we are able to imagine for the purposes of speaking about meaning turns out to be not only a signifying, but also a substantifying language as well, which freezes all intentional dynamism into a conceptual terminology."[30]

It is for this reason, it seems to me, that the purely classificatory uses of the actantial reduction (those which sort out narratives according to the various abstract categories dominant in them) are unsatisfactory. In fact Greimas'

---

[29] See for example Tzvetan Todorov, *Grammaire du Décaméron* (The Hague, 1969), pp. 46-50; or his "Poétique," in *Qu'est-ce que le structuralisme?* (Paris, 1968), esp. pp. 132-145.

[30] A. J. Greimas, *Du Sens* (Paris, 1970), p. 8.

model, like generative grammar, implies a double movement of analysis and synthesis, and constitutes what Sartre has called in a different connection a progressive-regressive method. The application of such a model is thus complete only when, having disengaged the basic deep structure, the analyst is then able to generate back up out of it not only the original text but all the other variants of which the model is susceptible as well. It is this generational mechanism which the Structuralists call a *combinatoire*. Ideally, therefore, such analysis presupposes a body or corpus of texts.

Within a given text, to be sure, the actantial reduction may serve a double function: horizontally, in the coordination of widely separated sections of such long and episodic forms as medieval romance, where it may prove useful to show that some particularly cryptic event towards the end is but a structural repetition—or inversion—of some more transparent initial one; vertically, in the demonstration of some identical mechanism at work on all the levels of discourse and expressing itself at some points as action, at others taking the form of an image, at still others being articulated as a psychological perception or a stylistic mannerism. In a later section we shall find Greimas proposing yet a different type of mechanism for such an ultimate nuclear cell of meaning itself, one which does away with the dramatic analogy in the present model.

A full-scale demonstration of the narrational *combinatoire* or story-generating mechanism—such as Greimas himself gives us in his studies of the Lithuanian version of the tale of the boy who wanted to learn fear[31]—involves a designation of its essential structural limits or *clôture*, and these may be described in an internal or an external way. Internal-

[31] See "La Quête de la peur" and especially "La Structure des actants du récit," in *Du Sens*, pp. 231-270.

ly, the structural limitation is nothing more than the total number of permutations and combinations inherently possible in the model in question; while the external limits are set by history itself, which pre-selects a certain number of structural possibilities for actualization, while proscribing others as inconceivable in the social and cultural climate of a given area. Thus, in Roman Catholic Lithuania, that logically possible variant of the tale in which the functions of paternity and of the sacred are superposed in a single actor or character must be excluded, since priests cannot be imagined as fathers; and more complicated solutions, in which the elder brother takes on the role of priest, or else the father confides the son to a surrogate who turns out to be a priest, are substituted.

Such a model may now be proposed for the study of all the works of a single writer (this is the domain of the older stylistics of Leo Spitzer and Jean-Pierre Richard, of which Greimas has given us an illustration in his work on Bernanos),[32] or for that of the varied works of a given, stylistically homogeneous period of literary history (where the material now involves the problems of periodization with which the art historians are concerned, as well as the kinds of homologies associated with the name of Lucien Goldmann).

Such a notion of a grammar of plots suggests that as in the history of ideas so in literature also we may see the work of a generation or of a period in terms of a given model (or basic plot paradigm), which is then varied and articulated in as many ways possible until it is somehow exhausted and replaced by a new one. Such a notion has the advantage of grounding the idea of novelty and of innovation (of which we have seen how essential a motor of the literary process the Formalists thought it to be) in the very structure

[32] See "Un Échantillon de description," in *Sémantique structurale*, pp. 222-256.

of the literary object itself, rather than in the psychology of its creators.

This is the sense of Barthes' paradoxical reversal in which he distinguishes diachrony from genuine history itself (which then becomes something like synchrony in its massive stability, in its *durée*). Speaking of the relationship of the "nouveau roman" to the engaged literature which it replaced, he says: "I would for my part be tempted to see in their alternation that purely formal process of the rotation of possibles which characterizes Fashion: there is exhaustion of one *parole* and transition to its antinomy: here *difference* is the motor, not of history, but of diachrony; history itself intervenes only when these micro-rhythms are perturbed, and when this kind of differential orthogenesis of forms has been unexpectedly blocked by a whole set of historical functions: it is what lasts that needs to be explained, not what 'rotates.' We might say allegorically that the (immobile) history of the alexandrian is more significant than the (transitory) fashion of trimeter: the longer forms persist, the more they approach that state of historical intelligibility which seems to me the object of all criticism today."[33]

What this means, of course, is that for the Structuralists the idea of a history of the objects or of the surface phenomena has been replaced with that of a history of models. We will return to this notion shortly.

5. In the preceding sections, we have seen two forms (which we have characterized as the phonological and the syntactical) of the structural analysis of the signifier; and it is to this dimension that the term *structure* most properly applies. It is this dimension also which Lacanian psychoanalysis calls the "symbolic order," and the idea has been influential in stimulating the kind of overestimation of the

---

[33] *Essais critiques*, p. 262.

dimension of the signifier which we will examine in the present section.

For Lacan, the Symbolic Order is that realm into which the child emerges, out of a biological namelessness, when he gradually acquires language. It is impersonal, or superpersonal, but is also that which permits the very sense of identity itself to come into being. Consciousness, personality, the subject, are, therefore, as we shall see shortly, secondary phenomena which are determined by the vaster structure of language itself, or of the Symbolic. Lacan chooses as an illustration of this process the rotating plot of Poe's *Purloined Letter*, in which, as in a repetition compulsion, the same event is reenacted twice, with the actors occupying different places in each version. The center of the story is the letter itself, which stands as a symbol of suspended or delayed communication in general, or of the autonomy of the signifier, which goes its own way, irrespective of the new meanings and new uses to which it is put, a free-floating object in the world, which soaks up ever new types of value. Hidden by the queen in the most open place available, a table in front of the king himself, it is brazenly lifted by the minister, from whom it is lifted by Dupin in turn from the most open place available, where the minister had hidden it. Thus the minister is himself a function of his situation with respect to the basic linguistic circuit. He, and the other characters, have no personality-substances of their own, no intrinsic being; rather, they derive their being from their positions with respect to the linguistic situation or the Symbolic Order itself.[34]

It is Lévi-Strauss, however, who reformulates this process in terms of a theory about the primacy of the signifier itself with respect to the signified. It is at this point that we

[34] See "Le Séminaire sur 'La Lettre volée,'" in *Écrits*, pp. 11-61.

can watch what was initially a method (the isolation of the signifier for purposes of structural analysis) slowly turn about into what amounts to a metaphysical presupposition as to the priority of the signifier itself, and this is the sense of his notion of the "surplus of signifier," first enunciated in connection with shamanism. For Lévi-Strauss, the shamanistic "cure" is to be attributed to the fact that the shaman offers, in his rituals and in the symbolic system of his mythology, an empty constellation of pure signifiers in which the free-floating unexpressed and inexpressible affectivity of the patient can suddenly articulate itself and find release. This is what he calls "symbolic efficacity": "the cure consists in rendering *thinkable* a situation at first given only in affective terms: rendering acceptable for the mind pain which the body refuses to tolerate."[35] It should be noted, however, that this analysis bears not on the content but rather on the form of the thought in question. It is not because the shaman offers a particularly satisfying type of magic explanation that the patient's mind is set at rest. Rather, this happens as a result of the availability of any kind of empty sign-system which would permit articulated thought (rather than wordless pain) in the first place.

This notion of the "surplus of signifier" has implications which greatly transcend the limits of the shamanistic situation (even though Lévi-Strauss, by comparing the process with psychoanalysis—a modern "shamanism"—has himself deliberately enlarged those limits), implications which involve our relationship with all new symbolic systems offered us. "Only the history of the symbolic function would permit us to do justice to this intellectual condition of man, which is that the universe never signifies enough, that thought always disposes of too many significations for the

[35] *Anthropologie structurale*, p. 217, italics mine.

quantity of objects to which it can attach them."[36] Henceforth the very process of thought itself becomes a relatively formal one. Our approach to Structuralism as a coherent system, for instance, does not so much involve the testing of theories and hypotheses as it does the learning of a new language, which we measure as we go along by the amount of translation we are able to effect out of the older terminology into the new. This is, incidentally, what explains the tremendous explosion of intellectual energies generated by a new system of this kind, and may serve, indeed, to define the notion of an intellectual movement as well. But only a small fraction of the intellectual energies thus released result in new theory. The overwhelming bulk of work done is simply a tireless process of translating all the old into the new terms, of endlessly reviving numbed perception and intellectual habit by forcing it through a new and unfamiliar intellectual procedure, by exhaustively applying the new intellectual paradigm.[37] When new discoveries are made, they result, I think, from the way in which the new model enlarges or refocuses corners of reality which the older terminology had left obscured, or had taken for granted. But such discovery is also assimilable to a process of translation.

The notion of a surplus of signifier is also useful in accounting for the changing function of literature itself. It is clear that even in the nineteenth century, writers were suppliers of products of a particular type. In this context the "style" of Dickens is if anything a form of packaging, a mannerism, an annoying or delightful "supplement" to those novel-products which it was his social role to furnish. But in modern times, it is clearly "style" itself, or "world,"

[36] *Ibid.*, pp. 202-203.
[37] The term is that of T. S. Kuhn, in *The Structure of Scientific Revolutions* (Chicago, 1962).

or world-view, which the novelist supplies. Little by little he abandons the practice of allowing it to come into being naturally through a series of separate books, and attempts to embody it all at once, in a single vast work which can no longer be called a "novel" as such. It becomes clear, therefore, that the contradictions involved in the notions of style or world-view or whatever are resolved if we understand that the novelist is in the process of elaborating a sign-system, a synchronic totality which we learn diachronically. And just as the very activity of the novelist himself changes direction when he realizes that he is the unconscious producer of a model or sign-system and now determines consciously to do so, so also the activity of the reader ceases to be that of a consumer of novels as such, and comes rather to resemble a series of religious conversions. The process of reading now involves the learning of a new sign-system, and we do not read a novel which happens to be by D. H. Lawrence; rather through that particular novel we approach the system of D. H. Lawrence as a whole, and we try it out, not as a representation of the real world, but rather as a surplus of signifier which permits us to rearticulate the formless, sprawling matter of the real world and of real experience into a new system of relations. It is an articulation as satisfying as any shaman's cure, and serves much the same function. (This notion of literature as model-building is, however, not the only one implicit in Structuralism, as we will see later on when we come to examine the aims of the group around *Tel Quel*.)

Ultimately, if the process of thought bears not so much on adequation to a real object or referent, but rather on the adjustment of the signified to the signifier (a tendency already implicit in Saussure's original concept of the sign), then the traditional notion of "truth" itself becomes outmoded. Barthes does not hesitate to propose a replacement

133

of it by the notion of a proof "by internal coherence": "if the rhetorical signified, in its unitary form, is nothing more than a construction, this construction must be coherent: the internal probability of the rhetorical signified is established in direct proportion to this coherence. Faced with the exigencies of a positive demonstration, or of real experimentation, this notion of internal coherence may seem a disappointing kind of 'proof': we are nonetheless more and more inclined to grant it heuristic if not scientific status; one branch of modern criticism aims at reconstructing creative universes by the thematic method (which is the method appropriate to immanent analysis), and in linguistics it is the coherence of a system (and not its 'use') which demonstrates its reality; and without wishing to underestimate their practical importance historically in the life of the modern world, the examination of their 'effects' is far from exhausting Marxist or psychoanalytic theory, which owe a decisive share of their 'probability' to their systematic coherence."[38] We should note that by "coherence" Barthes seems to have in mind the range and complexity of the sign-system in question also: its ability to absorb the largest quantity of signified possible, as well as its mere internal consistency as a system. It is in any case a somewhat different type of criterion from Greimas' notion of truth as an operation of a transcoding which we will examine at the end of this work.

The notion of the priority of the signifier (which as we have noted stands as a kind of metaphysical presupposition) finds its theoretical fulfillment in the Structuralist theory of models. For if, as we shall see shortly, the subject is a function of a more impersonal system or language-structure, then the various conscious positions and philosophical solutions devised by the subject are thereby devalued as well. In particular, Structuralism implies a thor-

[38] *Système de la mode*, p. 237.

oughgoing rejection of the pretensions of the Cartesian and Sartrean *cogito.*

Yet Structuralism does not for all that return to the absolute devaluation of conscious thought implicit in orthodox materialism, for which thought is nothing but a product of matter. Althusser has, more than anyone else, been responsible for the working out of a new Structuralist theory of models. The ingenuity of his solution may be emphasized by describing it as a reinsertion of the opposition of infrastructure and superstructure into the closed sphere of the mind itself, which is to say, within the superstructure. If, as we have seen above, philosophical positions are little more than systematic variations on a given paradigm or model, then what counts is not so much the individual position itself (a kind of superstructure within the superstructure), but rather the conceptual limits of the model in question, which thus becomes a kind of bed-rock of thought, of "theoretical praxis," where it functions as a type of infrastructure to the history of ideas. This reality of the model or of the ideational infrastructure Althusser calls the *problématique,* or problem-complex. The latter "determines" the thinking done in it in the sense in which it serves as an ultimate limitation on thought, on the conscious problems which thought poses itself, as well as on their solutions. This is, as we have seen above in a somewhat different context, the "clôture," or conceptual ceiling inherent in the model or paradigm which governs the thinking of a given generation; the implication is that a given generation will take its place as a whole within a given *problématique* and that the latter is at one with the historical moment itself. Genuine historical change will therefore be felt, not so much as development—for given a model, intellectual work will simply consist in its application or exploration—as a sudden replacement of an old problematics by a new one. It is thus, through the me-

135

diation of the problematic (and particularly at such moments of a shift in problematics, which, following Bachelard, Althusser calls a "coupure épistémologique"), that the world of the superstructure feels the geological shifts taking place in the world of real history outside it. This conception of historical change was already familiar to us in linguistic theory where Jakobson gave it the name of a mutation. The mutations in the superstructure are apparently not accessible to the analytical work itself, at least in terms of their own internal history; for they stand as incomprehensible results of earthquakes taking place somewhere outside. What is accessible to the theoretician is the relationship of the individual philosophical position or idea to the essential model or problem-complex on which it is based; this work of finding the model behind the idea is what Derrida has called a "deconstruction."

The originality of this Structuralist theory of models is to have reunited two areas that have historically had little enough to do with each other, namely official philosophy and the history of ideas; or, to put it another way, to lay a systematic and indeed philosophical basis for the method and practice of the history of ideas itself. Henceforth the latter is no longer an affair of trends and surface resemblances among ideas; it is rather a rigorous and controllable mode of research into the objective system behind ideas. As such, it has long been practiced by historians of science such as Bachelard or Koyré, whose raw material sorts itself out naturally into solutions or variations on the one hand and basic models on the other. One of the best illustrations of this Structuralist theory of models *avant la lettre* is T. S. Kuhn's *Structure of Scientific Revolutions*, developed independently and thus itself furnishing evidence for the existence of a structural or model-building *problématique* which governs the thinking of our generation in a way quite unrelated to any influence of Structuralism as an official theory or movement. The idealistic character of Althusser's solution may, however, be judged by comparing it to R. G. Collingwood's theory of "absolute presuppositions" which it so strikingly resembles. As a theory, however, it has the advantage of resolving the relatively fluid Saussurean relationship of *parole* to *langue* by making the latter (the model or the system), the situation to which the former is one possible response.

6. When now we reassess the position of consciousness, or the subject, in the light of this Structuralist emphasis on the priority of the system, or the *problématique*, or the Symbolic Order, it is inevitably the word "unconscious" which marks the area to be explored. It will have been clear already that for the Structuralists the unconscious stands to consciousness neither as matter to spirit, nor as the body to the mind, nor even primarily as the signified to the signifier. For Lacan the fact of concealment of unconscious phenomena from the knowledge of the subject "scarcely matters at all. . . . What this structure of the chain of signifiers reveals is that possibility which is mine—to the degree that its language is common to myself and to other subjects—to use it to say *something quite different* from what it says. A function more worthy of being underlined in the utterance than the act of disguising the (for the most part undefinable) thought of the subject: namely that of indicating the place of the subject in the search for truth."[39] The Lacanian unconscious is therefore not so much that dark inner reservoir of desire and instinct which used to be our image of the Freudian *id*, occasionally breaking into the realm of consciousness or insinuating its way there through the disguises of dreams. Rather, it is an absolute transparency, an order which is unconscious simply because it is infinitely vaster than our in-

[39] *Écrits*, pp. 504-505.

dividual minds, and because they owe their development to their positions within it. "It's wrong to think that the unconscious exists because of the existence of unconscious desire, of some obtuse, heavy, caliban, indeed animalic unconscious desire that rises up from the depths, that is primitive, and has to lift itself to the higher level of consciousness. Quite on the contrary, desire exists because there is unconsciousness, that is to say, language which escapes the subject in its structure and effects, and because there is always, on the level of language, something which is beyond consciousness, and it is there that the function of desire is to be located."[40] Psychic or affective depth is for Lacan, therefore, not located in the subject's relationship to his own inner depths (to his own unconscious or past or whatever), but, rather, as we shall see shortly, in his projective relationship to that Other implied by the linguistic circuit, and only then to himself, as to an alter-ego or mirror image.

Thus consciousness is something on the order of a "shifter" in linguistics (Jakobson's term for those words like personal pronouns which indicate the place of the sender of the message, and indeed shift their object of reference with the context).[41]

J'ai été mot parmi les lettres: So Denis Roche expresses this feeling of the subject, or of consciousness, as a kind of construction rather than a stable substance, as a locus of relationships rather than an ego in the older sense.[42] Thus, for some of the Structuralists, there is a kind of ethical reevaluation of the distance between neurosis and psychosis, which are now seen as two wholly distinct phenomena. Neurosis becomes a movement of repression which fails to rec-

[40] Quoted in *Qu'est-ce que le structuralisme?* pp. 252-253.
[41] See Wilden, *The Language of the Self*, pp. 183-184.
[42] Quoted by Marcelin Pleynet, in "La Poésie doit avoir pour but . . . ," *Tel Quel: Théorie d'ensemble* (Paris, 1968), p. 106.

ognize itself, and which attempts to stem the flight from one signifier to another by fixating on a single one, by choosing for itself in one form or another a transcendental signified, or a God. Psychosis, on the other hand, is simply a writing out of all the possible variations of a given paradigm: "It is known that for Freud the various forms that paranoia can take all result from various ways of contradicting one basic proposition: 'I love him'. . . . The delirium (or text) of the paranoiac, and the themes which derive from it, thus depend on the manner in which the grammatical form of the enunciation is established. . . . If Freud gives us to understand that the perversions of voyeurism/exhibitionism and those of sadism/masochism are opposing forms of the same instinct, then perhaps we are authorized to see in them various ways of transforming a given enunciation. The unity of sadism and masochism would thus result from the priority of the text and of the grammatical function over anything that might appeal to some basic 'nature' or mysterious determination of the subject. There is no sadistic or masochistic nature, only the particular effects of a single enunciation whose terms shift places."[43]

The most scandalous aspect of Structuralism as a movement—its militant anti-humanism, as found both in Marxists (Althusser) and in anti-Marxists (Foucault) alike—must be understood conceptually as a refusal of the older categories of human nature and of the notion that man (or human consciousness) is an intelligible entity or field of study in himself.[44] From an ethical or psychological point of

[43] Jean-Louis Baudry, "Écriture, fiction, idéologie," in *Tel Quel: Théorie d'ensemble*, pp. 145-146. The reference is to Freud's 1911 essay "On the Mechanism of Paranoia."

[44] "In our time, and Nietzsche is still there to mark the point of inflexion from a distance, it is not so much the absence or the death of God which is affirmed, but the end of man. . . . More than the death of God—or rather in the wake of this death and in profound

view, however, it must be pointed out that such a valorization of the Symbolic Order, with its accompanying humiliation of the old-fashioned subject or personal and individual
consciousness, is by no means as unproblematical as some
of its spokesmen have given us to understand. In particular,
if the Symbolic Order is the source of all meaning, it is also
and at the same time the source of all cliché, the very
fountainhead of all those more debased "meaning-effects"
which saturate our culture, the very seat and locus of the
inauthentic in Heidegger's sense. This is an aspect of the
doctrine which has perhaps been obscured by the emphasis
in structural research on pre-capitalistic and indeed pre-in-
dividualistic materials such as folklore and myth, causing us
to forget that the equivalents in our own society for the
"myth" or "pensée sauvage" of cold societies or primitive
cultures are neither Joyce nor Husserl, but rather the best-
seller and the advertising slogan, the Barthean "mytho-
logie."[45] So it is that our possession by language, which
"writes" us even as we imagine ourselves to be writing it, is
not so much some ultimate release from bourgeois subjectiv-
ism, but rather a limiting situation against which we must
struggle at every instant. Thus the Symbolic Order can only
be said to represent a psychic conquest from the vantage
point of that imaginary stage which it supersedes: for the
death of the subject, if it might be supposed to characterize
the collective structure of some future socialist world, is

---

correlation with it, what Nietzsche's thought announces is the end
of his murderer; the bursting of the human face into laughter and
the return of masks. . . ." (Michel Foucault, *Les Mots et les choses*
[Paris, 1966], pp. 396-397.)

[45] See for a particularly rich study of the origins and formation of
collective superstition and debased consciousness in the Symbolic Order, Georges Auclair, *Le Mana quotidien: structures et fonctions de la
chronique des faits divers* (Paris, 1970), especially p. 239.

fully as characteristic of the intellectual, cultural, and psychic decay of post-industrial monopoly capitalism as well.

We may, however, choose to see this essential theme of Structuralism, not so much as an intrinsic discovery in its own right, but rather as a kind of motivation for some more basic tendency in structural research, namely the emphasis on decoding and decipherment.

Indeed, the characteristic imagery—geological upheaval, archeology of knowledge—insists repeatedly on this characteristic of Structuralist activity as a going beyond the surface of the given, as a deduction of the existence, behind the phenomenon, of phenomena or forces of a wholly different nature altogether. No one has better described this passion for decipherment than Lévi-Strauss himself, when, speaking of "the intense curiosity which from childhood had driven me towards geology," he evokes "the pursuit, along the flank of a *causse* in Languedoc, of the line of contact between two geological layers. . . . Every countryside offers an immense disorder in which you are free to choose the meaning you wish to impose on it. But, over and beyond agricultural experimentation, geographical accident, avatars of history and prehistory, is that meaning not grave among all others which precedes, commands and in large measure explains the others themselves? That pale blurred line, that almost imperceptible difference in the form and consistency of the debris of rock, bears witness to the fact that there where today I see arid soil, two oceans had once upon a time succeeded one another. In the attempt to follow the evidence of their millenary stagnation—continuing heedless of paths and barriers alike through all obstacles in the way, across abrupt cliffs, landslides, brush, cultivated fields—you seem utterly senseless in your movements. Yet this insubordination has as its aim the reestablishment of a

141

higher meaning (*maître-sens*), one undoubtedly faint and distant, but of which each of the others is but a partial or deformed transposition. Let the miracle take place, as it sometimes happens; let on one side and the other of the secret rift appear two green plants of different species, each of which has chosen the most propitious soil; let there be glimpsed at the very same moment within the rock itself two ammonites of two different orders of complicated involutions, each attesting in its own fashion to a leap of several dozen millennia: and suddenly time and space are mingled; the living diversity of the instant juxtaposes and perpetuates the ages. . . . I feel myself bathed by a deeper intelligibility in which ages and places reply to each other and speak languages reconciled at last."[46]

This attachment to the essentially cryptographic nature of reality explains why Lévi-Strauss insists that, in distinction to history (whose object is conscious action), the object of anthropology is the unconscious and its systems, which it deciphers from the data at its disposal.[47] It also explains the theoretical appeal of both Marx and Freud, not only for Lévi-Strauss himself, but also for Structuralism in general; for Freudian theory represents "an application to individual man of a method of which geology constitutes the canon";[48] and both Freudianism and Marxism share with geology a conviction "that understanding consists in the *reduction* of one type of reality to another; that true reality is never what is manifest on the surface, and that the nature of truth may be measured by the degree to which it tries to elude you . . . that the passage between the two orders [of lived experience and of reality] is discontinuous; that in order to reach the real, one must repudiate the existential, only to rein-

---

[46] Lévi-Strauss, *Tristes tropiques* (Paris, 1955), pp. 48-49.
[47] *Anthropologie structurale*, p. 25.
[48] *Tristes tropiques*, p. 49.

tegrate it later on in an objective synthesis from which all sentimentality has been eliminated."[49]

We here therefore find renewed that antagonism which we have more fully described elsewhere[50] between a philosophy of the symbol and a philosophy of the sign; between a viewpoint for which the signifier and the signified, the various sign-systems among each other, and indeed the sign and its referent, are somehow homologous with each other, and one which insists on the basic discontinuity between these levels, on the arbitrary nature, not only of the sign, but even of the sign-system itself. In this context we might well reverse our conceptual priorities and understand the Freudian notion of the unconscious simply as one of the most influential versions of such a doctrine of the arbitrary nature of the sign, or, to use Lacan's expression, as the "bar" which separates signifier (S) from signified (s) in the well-known formula for the psyche:[51] $\frac{S}{s}$. It is in any case clear that in the context of literary analysis both concepts—that of an unconscious and that of an arbitrary relationship between the levels of discourse—are essentially figures for an interpretive operation of a particular type, in which a first naive reading is replaced by a second, analytic one, and where there is foreseen, and indeed prescribed, some basic discontinuity between the two from the very outset. Thus where the second reading of the older, "intrinsic" criticism remained faithful to that first impression which it merely sought to articulate and bring to more precise consciousness, the newer structural interpretation is directed, during the second reading, to just those non-functioning and apparently insignificant elements which had

---

[49] *Ibid.*, p. 50.
[50] See my *Marxism and Form*, pp. 222-225.
[51] See for example *Écrits*, pp. 515ff.

been disregarded during the "natural" reading of the text. Wholly disengaged and dispassionate, it now takes inventory of the text much as the analyst takes inventory of the dream of someone else: noting, for instance, that where the hero has a domineering mother (and a string of divorces), the spy has a sister who at one moment in the masquerade is called upon to play his wife. The whole force of the surprise inherent in such interpretation (which shows, let us say, that what we had taken to be a thriller and a love story in reality proved to be a message about two different kinds of kinship patterns) depends on our having neglected during our first reading of the work those minute signifying elements from which the fundamental binary oppositions are then evolved.

Ultimately, of course, the doctrine of some essential heterogeneity between signifier and signified will, with Foucault and Derrida, become the instrument of a radical critique of the Western philosophical and metaphysical tradition, which has always emphasized the identity between experience and knowledge, between language and thought, and which has carried out its tasks beneath the sign of the ideal of total presence, the mirage of the *logos* as the ultimate univocal concept.[52] It is for this reason that what began as the projection of a linguistic model based primarily on the spoken dimension of language will find its ultimate avatar in a theory of script.

3

1. The study of the dimension of the signified is what has been called (as opposed to a linguistics) a structural or semiological semantics: it is not, for all that, an any less profoundly paradoxical undertaking. The very notion of a

[52] An earlier expression of such a critique had been worked out by Lucien Sebag in *Marxisme et structuralisme* (Paris, 1964).

signified as such would seem to presuppose that it had already been articulated into a system of signifiers in its own right, that is to say, dissolved *qua* signified and reorganized or assimilated into a sign-system of its own. Before the organizing and enabling act of speech itself, we cannot think of the signified as being anything more than an "undefined mass of concepts, which could be compared to a huge jellyfish, with uncertain articulations and contours."[53] To speak of it any way at all, even to isolate the signified as such for purposes of description, would seem to imply that it had already found some determinate type of organization, or in other words that what we had taken to be a signified, what indeed had been a signified on one level and with respect to one particular type of signifier, turned out on another to be itself a signifying system with respect to some lower level of the signified, in a kind of infinite regression. We cannot at this point do any more than indicate such profound structural dissymmetry in the couple signifier/signified, the first of which seems able to exist as a kind of free-floating autonomous organization, while the other is never visible directly to the naked eye.

2. It is, however, an ambiguity which makes out the privileged place of Roland Barthes in the Structuralist movement; for in that peculiar distribution of roles and specialties which characterizes Structuralism, and in which Lévi-Strauss secures anthropology, and Lacan and Althusser are charged with the reinterpretations of Freud and Marx respectively, in which Derrida and Foucault assure the rewriting, the one of the history of philosophy, the other of the history of ideas, while Greimas and Todorov are at work transforming linguistics and literary criticism proper into sciences, a situation in which Merleau-Ponty, had he

[53] Barthes, *Système de la mode*, p. 236. The image is Saussure's: *Cours de linguistique générale*, p. 155.

lived, might have assumed the central chair of philosophy itself, it would seem that the role left to devolve upon Roland Barthes is essentially that of sociologist. It is Barthes, indeed, who pursues what is basically a sociological investigation of the imaginary objects and culture-institutions of a civilization saturated with advertising and ideology: in his *Mythologies*, that marvelous picture-book of the pinups from the news of the day (boxing matches, somebody's new *Phèdre*, Billy Graham at the Vel d'hiver, the myth of the Guide bleu or of steak-frites, the strip tease, the new model cars); in his study, in *Système de la mode*, of the structure of fashion; in his reading, in *L'Empire des signes*, of that immense scroll or text which is written in characters of human flesh and formal gardens, of sliding screens and student helmets, tea ceremonies and transistorized radios, across the length and breadth of the Japanese archipelago; in his theory, finally, of the literary sign and of literature as a social institution.

Yet Barthes is of course primarily thought of as a literary critic. Our somewhat fanciful characterization of him above will be primarily useful to the degree to which it points to some deeper ambiguity in the very structure of the literary work itself, to something in the verbal construction of literature which allows it to be assimilated to, and even perhaps to serve as a paradigm for, other, more properly sociological sign-systems. This will be clearest if we isolate the type of signified with which Barthes has to deal, the privileged object of his research, or to use an older language, his obsessional themes or raw materials: for, as we have already seen, only a signified of a very distinct internal structure can be thus isolated from its signifier for experimental purposes.

What characterizes the most typical object of Barthes' perception is, it seems to me, a set of double markings in the thing signified, a structure of double functions irreducible to each other and incommensurable, operating at wholly different levels. It is as though only such an ambiguously structured signified, which seems to project two different types of signifiers and to lie at their intersection, can make itself felt as a kind of density and resistance beneath the transparency of the signs. This double structure is explicitly described in Barthes' recent work: the object of fashion, the vestimentary article (at least insofar as it is described in the fashion magazines) signifies at one and the same time High Society and Fashion itself. Each item has two possible uses, which can be exercised simultaneously: on the one hand, it permits an imaginary identification with the rich and their way of life, and on the other it serves as a sign of fashion, momentarily embodying in itself all of what is currently fashionable.

Yet the same double structure was implicit in Barthes' earlier works as well. In the book on Michelet, for instance, Barthes postulates two simultaneous motivations for the historical text at any given point: the linear and official narrative of history itself (which Barthes leaves aside); and a kind of *combinatoire* or interplay of existential themes and motifs, an intersection of horizontal and vertical dimensions, to use a figure characteristic of Barthes in this period; while in *Sur Racine* the critic's practice generates a tension between the play as social ritual, as conventional spectacle, between classical language as an institutionalized sign of the social order, and those deeper, private zones of Freudian obsession, of symbolic fulfillment and psychic space. Barthes' most recent studies of *Sade, Fourier, Loyola*, indeed, mark a return to the description of such tensions between the sign and the body: for all three of these apparently heterogeneously juxtaposed authors attempted to create new languages or sign-systems (the mathematical com-

147

binations of Sade's orgies, Loyola's mechanical recipes for the stimulation of inner and theatrical visions, Fourier's immense classification system of the drives and their harmonious interaction), while at the same time such sign-systems are empty, and call out in all three cases for investment by wordless physiological content or *hylé*.

But it is in S/Z, his commentary on Balzac's *Sarrasine*, that Barthes discovers the most explicit manifestation of such a double structure, which now takes the form of a story within a story. Barthes' study is as much a meditation on a fascinating object as it is the development of a critical thesis. For Balzac's novella speaks to us at once of itself and of its subject-matter, of art and of desire, both of which are present, with reversed emphasis, in the frame and in the actual tale alike. In the frame, the narrator tells a tale in order to seduce his listener; while within the tale itself an artist is destroyed by his desire, leaving only its representation—a statue and a portrait of Zambinella—behind in the final catastrophe. This passion is narcissism and castration: the infatuated artist in reality sees his own image in the castrate with whom he falls in love, so that the gesture of symbolic castration or sexual renunciation is here given to be the very source of artistic productivity, just as it turns out elsewhere in the story to be the very source of the Lanty family's mysterious fortune (Zambinella's success as prima donna). The fable thus has something to say about the origins of classical art and the origins of capitalization and their relationship to each other; yet it does not leave the frame within which it is told intact. Rather, it contaminates teller and listener alike, who separate at its close, in the desexualized and desexualizing atmosphere, without having consummated their desire.

With such a work, we clearly have to do with what Greimas would call the superposition of a teleological and a communicational axis: one *isotopie* or narrational level having to do with desire for an object, the other with the emission of a message. The reversal which takes place—in which the message replaces the object and becomes as it were a message about a lost object—is, as we shall see shortly, profoundly emblematic of Structuralist interpretation in general, and may fittingly be inserted here, like the *composition en abyme* of Dutch painting, into a study of it.

Once the signified has been thus isolated for study (if indeed we are able to so isolate it), by the very nature of things it turns into a sign-system in its own right. As Saussure himself warns us: *"whether we examine the signified or the signifier,* language involves neither ideas nor sounds which would preexist the linguistic system, but only conceptual or phonic differences which have resulted from that system."[54] We may conclude that insofar as we can talk about the signified at all, either it still bears traces of its organization by the signifier, or else the analyst has himself provisionally organized it into a new sign-system, in order to make it visible to us.

Thus we find again within the signified that structure of differential opposition and identity within difference that served to organize the signifier or language itself. In Barthes' study of Michelet, for instance—even though the principle is not yet formulated explicitly there—we find an organization of the essential themes by pairs of binary oppositions: grace and justice, Christianity and revolution; on the one hand, groupings of enchantment, narcosis, the sterile, "la mort sèche," and, on the other, blood, woman, the hero, energy. These combinations may at any given moment reach a high order of complexity (and it would have been interesting to watch the later Barthes rework them into semio-

<hr />

[54] Quoted by Derrida in "La Différance," *Tel Quel: Theorie d'ensemble,* p. 49, italics mine.

logical equations), but essentially they form what Saussure would have called a vertical level of association which is constantly in play along the syntagmatic axis of the narrative itself. Thus, for Barthes, the key episodes are heightened and intensified by these binary oppositions: "For Michelet, Blood is the cardinal substance of History. Look at the death of Robespierre for example: two types of blood there face each other: one poor, dry, so thin it needs an artificial blood supplement in the form of galvanic energy; the other, that of the women of Thermidor (solar month of history), is a superlative blood, uniting all the characteristics of superb sanguinity: the warm, the red, the unclothed, the too-well-nourished. These two types of blood stare at each other. Then the Woman-Blood devours the Priest-Cat. . . . This whole meeting between the dry (electrical) and the full (feminine) in the death of Robespierre . . . is ordered in Michelet like an act of carnal humiliation, that of a chilly man, half undone in filthy linens, jaw hanging down, *looked at* by opulent women, scarlet with velvet, with nourishment and with jubilation, which is to say the very type of the sterile exposed and sold out to triumphant heat."[55]

The later evolution of Barthes makes it clear that what must at first have looked (even to Barthes himself) like a study in psychological or existential *themes*[56] was in reality the sketch of a type of discourse, that of the body itself. Michelet is indeed particularly rich in this physical dimension, in the peculiar heightened sensitivity or migraine-like nausea which he feels before the physical humors of his historical actors: "Michelet's adjective is unique; it marks a touch, an ideal palpation which has located the elementary substance of the body in question and can no longer con-

[55] Roland Barthes, *Michelet par lui-même* (Paris, 1965), pp. 105, 87.
[56] *Ibid.*, pp. 5 and 86.

ceive of the man under any different qualification, after the fashion of a natural epithet. Michelet says: the dessicated Louis XV, the cold Sieyès, and engages through these denominations his own judgment on the essential movements of matter itself: liquefaction, stickiness, the void, dessication, electricity."[57] The place of this vertical dimension was for the older critical terminology the unconscious, where it is now the body: and for Barthes indeed the body is the very source of style itself as a private phenomenon, as obsession and "the decorative voice of unknown, secret flesh."[58] But in reality there is no contradiction between these two formulations if we understand both the unconscious and the body as essential forms of the signified itself.

There is a sense in which all sensory perception already constitutes a kind of organization into language. It is this more than anything else, no doubt, which explains the sympathy of Merleau-Ponty in his last years for the then emergent Structuralism. Imagine the way in which, for a trained naturalist, the disorderly undergrowth of thickets and bushes pressing in upon each other sort themselves out into order, the peculiar outlines of each type of leaf standing as a visible sign and mark of their determinate species; imagine the way in which a wholly unfamiliar landscape would offer itself to such knowledgeable perception as a kind of language the words of which were not yet known, an order already making itself felt through the clear forms of the vegetation, where for a layman there would be nothing but confused and jumbled vistas of space. This is, no doubt, what the German Romantics dimly felt when they developed their mystique of a language of organic nature; it is also the secret rationale behind Bachelardian analysis, which Barthes occasionally practices, but as to whose status he

---

[57] *Ibid.*, p. 82.
[58] *Le degré zéro de l'écriture*, pp. 14-15.

seems uncertain:[59] "Bachelard was no doubt right to see in water the opposite of wine: mythically this is so; sociologically, at least today, it is less certain; economic or historical circumstances have shifted this role to milk. Milk is now the veritable anti-wine . . . the opposite of fire by all its molecular density, by the creamy and therefore sopitive nature of its surface folds; wine is mutilating, surgical, it transmutes and brings to birth; milk is cosmetic, it unites, seals over, restores. Moreover its purity, associated with childlike innocence, is a proof of force, non-revulsive, non-congestive, one which is calm, white, lucid, on an equal footing with the real."[60] For just as the dimension of the signified can never be completely isolated in a pure state, so also it is vain to attempt to distinguish between Nature and Culture on this level, and to separate what belongs to a genuine Bachelardian "psychoanalysis of matter" from what may stand as a cultural or ideological myth at work on the level of perception itself. As enormously influential and suggestive as Bachelard's own work was, what it lacked above all else was a theory of language: assimilating sense perception to linguistic articulation without realizing that in one way or another, all perceptual systems are already languages in their own right.

Yet it is this vertical depth of the signified, which seems grounded in the wordless and the physical itself, in complexion and organic humor, that accounts for the peculiar density of Barthes' own language as well: for his style is an attempt to lend a second voice to the signified, to articulate

---

[59] "Sometimes, even here in these mythologies, I have cheated: weary of constantly working on the evaporation of the real, I have occasionally begun to thicken it excessively, to find in it a surprising compacity, one which I myself found delectable, and have given several substantialist psychoanalyses of mythical objects" (*Mythologies*, p. 267, n. 30).

[60] *Ibid.*, pp. 85-86.

its organization before it finds its final and official version in the primary signifier itself, in the text. His is a style of nouns and adjectives, of neologisms, as he is well aware: "The concept is the constitutive element of myth: if I want to decipher myths, I must be able to name concepts. The dictionary furnishes some: Goodness, Charity, Health, Humanity, etc. But by definition, since it's the dictionary that supplies them, those concepts cannot be historical. What I need most frequently are ephemeral concepts, linked to limited contingencies: neologisms are at this point inevitable. China is one thing, the idea which a French petty bourgeois not so long ago had about it is something else again: there can be no other name, for this characteristic mixture of little bells, rickshaws and opium dens, than that of *sinity*."[61] The neologism is therefore that which names the substance, just as adjectives (sopitive, dry-electrical) have as their function the attachment of a given detail to the larger structure of the signified as a whole, just as the definite articles and capital letters articulate the objects into a new relationality by their insistence and iteration ("As language, the singularity of Garbo was of a conceptual, that of Audrey Hepburn of a substantial, type of order. Garbo's face is Idea, Hepburn's is Event."[62]).

Ultimately the aim of this style is the bringing into being of new and somehow synthetic entities out of the surface data of the text, as in the following evocation of the Neronian *caress* (from the discussion of *Britannicus*): "Nero is he who enwraps, because enwrapment does not know death until it has been consummated. This 'gliding' has a funereal substitute in poison. Blood is a noble, theatrical matter, the sword is an instrument of rhetorical death; but Nero wishes the pure and simple effacement of Britannicus, not

---

[61] *Ibid.*, p. 228.   [62] *Ibid.*, p. 79.

his spectacular undoing; like the Neronian caress, poison insinuates itself, like the caress also it only yields effects, not means; in this sense caress and poison are part of an immediate order, in which the distance from the project to the crime is absolutely diminished; Neronian poison is in any case rapid poison, its advantage lies, not in delay, but in nudity, in the refusal of bloody theater."[63] Thus, in this sumptuous and perverse style, in which the ideas are not so much unfolded as laterally evoked by the very materiality of vocabulary itself, what comes into being are unstable conceptual entities, the very forms of the signified itself, as they darken the other side of language, constantly dissolving and reforming before our eyes. The very function of the style's artificiality is to announce itself as a metalanguage, to signal by its own impermanency the essential formlessness and ephemerality of the object itself.

Barthes had in his earlier work already evolved a theory to account for the phenomenon of double-functionality which we have described above. This theory (known as that of the "literary sign," where the term is to be understood in a far more limited way than in Saussure) is expressed in his most influential theoretical work, *Writing Degree Zero*. Literature, as a conventionalized activity—as what he will later call an "institutionalization of subjectivity"—is the very prototype of those ambiguous double-functioning substances which both have a meaning and wear a label at the same time: "I am a fifth-form student in a French lycée; I open my latin grammar and read in it the following sentence, borrowed from Aesop or Phaedrus: *quia ego nominor leo*. I stop and think: there is something ambiguous about this proposition: on the one hand, its words have a clear enough meaning: *for my name is lion*. And on the other hand the

[63] *Sur Racine*, pp. 91-92. This is one of the passages singled out for derision by Picard in *Nouvelle critique ou nouvelle imposture?*

154

sentence is obviously there to convey something else to me: to the degree that it is addressed to me, to a fifth-form student, it tells me clearly: I am an example of grammar intended to illustrate the rule about the agreement of attributes."[64] Thus literature in its complexity of structure, is a construction to a higher power than the transparency of the normal object of linguistic study: in it the ordinary signifier/signified relationship is complicated by yet another type of signification which bears on the nature of the code itself. Thus each literary work, above and beyond its own determinate content, also signifies literature in general. Like the Latin sentence, above and beyond what it actually does mean, it also says: I am Literature, and in so doing, identifies itself for us as a literary product, and involves us in that particular and historical social activity which is the consumption of literature. Thus, in the nineteenth century novel, the *passé simple* and the narrative third person are both signs the function of which is to warn us that we are in the presence of official literary narration; and these peculiar markings or "signs" are somehow different in their nature from the general body of linguistic prescriptions at a given period in the history of the language (which are somehow "on this side of literature"), as well as from what we have described as style above, which is "almost beyond literature: images, an allure, a vocabulary born from the body and the past of the writer himself."[65]

Thus the history of these literary "signs" would afford the possibility of a historical mode of examining literature radically different from the history of language, on the one hand, or the evolution of styles, on the other. Rather, it would constitute a kind of history of the literary institution itself, insofar as the literary "sign" reveals the obligatory distance

[64] *Mythologies*, pp. 222-223.
[65] *Le degré zéro de l'écriture*, p. 14.

155

that obtains at any given period between the reader and the literary product and between the writer and the product as well. This is how Barthes sums up his findings, and evokes the trajectory of such a history of signs: "First an artisanal consciousness of literary manufacture, pushed to painful scruple, to the torment of the impossible (Flaubert); then the heroic will to mingle in a single written substance both literature and the thinking about literature (Mallarmé); then the hope of succeeding in eluding literary tautology by ceaselessly postponing literature until tomorrow, so to speak, by indicating at great length that you are about to write and then transforming this very declaration into literature itself (Proust); then the attack on literary good faith by the deliberate and systematic multiplication of an infinite number of meanings of the word-object without ever pausing at any univocal signified (surrealism); finally, the reverse of this process, a rarefication of meanings, to the point of hoping to obtain some *density* in literary language, a kind of whiteness of writing (but not an innocence): I am thinking of the work of Robbe-Grillet."[66]

This theory is essentially a further elaboration and working out of the basic position of Sartre in *What Is Literature?* where it is by its structure that the work poses and indeed chooses its basic audience. Here it is the literary "sign" which essentially chooses the reader, and there are a whole complex of signs or indications through which a best-seller identifies itself to its clientele, through which a communist novel reveals its identity to its particular public, through which official, avant-garde literature announces at the same time its nature and the type of reading and distance it requires. But the methodological difference between Barthes and Sartre is that the former distinguishes between a selec-

[66] *Essais critiques*, pp. 106-107.

tion by content (which was essentially the burden of Sartre's analysis) and the operation of these peculiar "signs" which in themselves mean nothing (thus the *passé simple* does not govern a different mode of the past from other past tenses, it merely signals the presence of "literariness"). This relational language (at its crudest often little more than a matter of recognizable in-group vocabulary) is what has often been described as "tone" in Anglo-American criticism; however, the latter, convinced of the traditional homogeneity of its public, never attempted to distinguish radically between such a sign-system and actual style itself (which for Barthes has something of the function of poetry in the Sartrean scheme in that it comes closest, in its elimination of signs, to a pure density as a language-object).

The originality of Barthes' theory was to have permitted a somewhat different outcome than that envisioned in Sartre's book. For Sartre, a genuine literature can be achieved only when its public is everyone, when through the process of social revolution the virtual and the real publics are one and the same. For Barthes also the literary "sign" is the object of a profound political and ethical disgust:[67] insofar as it marks my affiliation with a given social group, it sig-

[67] "From an ethical point of view, what bothers one about myth is precisely that its form is motivated. For if there is such a thing as a 'health' of language, it is founded on the arbitrary quality of the sign. What disgusts in myth is the recourse to a false nature, the *luxury* of significative forms, as in those objects which decorate their usefulness with a natural appearance. The will to burden signification with all the justification of nature itself provokes a kind of nausea: the myth is too rich, and what is excessive in it is precisely its motivation. This disgust is the same as what I feel before arts which hesitate between *physis* and *anti-physis*, using the first as an ideal, and the second as a kind of reserve. Ethically, there is a kind of baseness involved in playing both sides against the middle." (*Mythologies*, p. 234, n. 7.) It should be unnecessary to add that what Barthes calls "myths" here (the modern ideological objects studied in his mythologies) have nothing to do with those primitive myths studied by Lévi-Strauss.

nifies the exclusion of all the others also—in a world of classes and violence, even the most innocuous group-affiliation carries the negative value of aggression with it. Yet the objective situation is such that I cannot but belong to groups of some kind, even if they turn out to be groups which wish to abolish the existence of groups: by the very fact of my existence, I am guilty of the exclusion of others from the groups in which I am involved. Thus the use of the "sign" is a kind of historical fatality, and marks my fall into, and acceptance of, the world of classes. It is for this reason that literature, in our time, is essentially an impossible enterprise, a self-unravelling process. At the same time that it poses its own universality, the very words it uses to do so signal their complicity with that which makes universality unrealizable.

Yet in Barthes, the concept of the literary "sign"—while continuing to project that ultimate utopia of style foreseen by Sartre—offers at least the logical possibility of another, more provisional solution as well. This solution is the forcible eradication of literary "signs" from the work itself or, in other words, the practice of a kind of "white writing," the access to a kind of "zero degree" of literary language in which neither author nor public could be felt present, in which an austere neutrality and stylistic asceticism would be charged with the absolution of the guilt inherent in the practice of literature.[68] This state would be, it seems to me, the equivalent of a kind of absolute solitude in the realm of social life, in which a rigorous political logic might dictate the suppression of everything (both within and without the personality) which links us with the repressive social institutions.

[68] The notion of a zero degree or negative ending (in the declension of a word) had already been appropriated, in a different way, by the Formalists. See above, pp. 63-64.

The value of this concept may be measured against its speculative quality, for at the period at which Barthes wrote there did not yet exist any examples of "white writing" as such. His principal contemporary example, Camus' *Stranger*, has come to seem to us stylized and rhetorical, the very type of writing charged with signs. (In another sense, of course, this judgment only serves to confirm Barthes' intuition of the impossibility of literature: for writing cannot *stay* white, what began by being a blankness of manner little by little turns around into a mannerism, absence of sign becomes a sign itself.) Since that time, Robbe-Grillet has come to be felt as a more thoroughgoing and convincing embodiment of an elimination of signs, at least insofar as his work is based on the disappearance of the subject; but I would be tempted to prefer the more politically charged versions of such stylistic neutrality that one finds in the novels of Uwe Johnson, let us say, or in Georges Pérec's *Les Choses*.

The changeover in Barthes' general positions (I hesitate to call it a *coupure épistémologique*) may be identified by a replacement (although not a repudiation) of this limited theory of the literary sign by a more complex one derived from Hjelmslev's distinction between "connotation" and "metalanguage." In both these linguistic phenomena, two distinct sign-systems are involved, stand somehow in relationship to each other. But a metalanguage takes the other language as its object, and functions as a signifier to the other language, which is thus its signified. Thus Barthean commentary is metalanguage in that it abstracts the structure of another more primary language, such as that of Michelet or that of Racine, and makes it available in a new and different form (in which, as we have shown, the neologisms function as a reminder that we have to do with a metalanguage rather than a primary, or object-language).

In the phenomenon of connotation, on the other hand, in the limited and technical sense which Hjelmslev gives the word, it is the whole body of one language system which stands as a signifier for some more basic signified. The primary language system really thus has two signifieds: its regular content, which we receive consecutively as the text continues, and a second overall message sent us by the form as a whole. Thus a critique of Flaubert's style would take the form of a metalanguage; but the totality of Flaubert's own words forms a connotational system of its own, in that it signifies Literature, and tells us over and over again: I am literature of an artisanal type, I am the specialized work of the stylistic artisan.

We will return to the notion of metalanguage later on. For the moment, suffice it to say that as useful as the assimilation of the restricted theory of the literary sign to the more generalized theories of linguistics may be, I cannot but feel that the individual manifestations of the phenomenon of connotation were more immediately available to us when we could think of them precisely as individual signs and markings rather than as some global message or content. Yet the most serious consequence of the changeover lies elsewhere: the new terminology rules out the very possibility of a zero degree of signs, and that possibility—a utopian one, no doubt—nonetheless retained its political implications. It is an oversimplification to think of Structuralism (as opposed, let us say, to Sartrean existentialism and *engagement*) as an apolitical phenomenon, an ideological reflexion of Gaullist France. This is, for one thing, to forget its militant left-wing organized around the review *Tel Quel*. It would seem, nonetheless, that with the new institutional orientation of Structuralism and its assimilation into the French university system, the older option of an absolute solitude is lost, and the essentially political tension of the concept of a zero degree tends to cool into old-fashioned scientific objectivity: what was once a differential lack, felt as such, now little by little becomes simply a non-registered, non-functioning absence.

3. A basic step in the disentanglement of signified from signifier—in the postulating of some deeper and independent layer of which the signifier would itself be a kind of translation—is taken when we slip almost insensibly from the concept of the signifier as a series of binary oppositions to that for which the signifier is an attempt to *resolve* such oppositions, now thought of as contradictions. We may leave unanswered the question of whether Barthes' double objects might not themselves be seen anew in such terms as these. It is, indeed, primarily in the work of Lévi-Strauss that we watch such a reformulation at work. Thus, to recall the analysis of the Oedipus myth once again, the double opposition which structured the narrative (overestimated vs. underestimated, family vs. earth) proved itself to be the expression of a more basic antinomy for the primitive mind, namely, how one man could be the product of two people rather than that of the earth alone. It is at this point that Lévi-Strauss postulates his well-known equation with multiple variables as the form through which a given mythic material seeks to transform a problematical starting point into a satisfactory solution.[69]

Yet what is felt as an antinomy on the level of pure thought, on the level of the superstructure, may be seen as

[69] Cf. *Anthropologie structurale*, pp. 252-253. For demonstrations of this formula I must refer the reader to the excellent "Structural Models in Folklore," of Elli-Kaija Köngäs and Pierre Maranda (*Midwest Folklore*, Vol. XII, No. 3, 1962, pp. 133-192); and see Louis Marin, *Sémiotique de la Passion* (Paris: Bibliothèque des Sciences religieuses, 1971), pp. 107-110; as well as my own "Max Weber: A Psychostructural Analysis," in *New Writings in Humanist Sociology*, ed. Stanford M. Lyman and Richard H. Brown (Princeton, forthcoming).

a contradiction when we look at it from the point of view of the concrete social whole itself. Lévi-Strauss' dissection of the Oedipus myth was hypothetical precisely because he made abstraction of its social context (and we may recall that Lévi-Strauss invokes the authority of Engels for the way in which anthropologists describe the infrastructure in terms of marriage pattern and tribal structure rather than of technique and economic organization).

This is what happens when Lévi-Strauss turns his attention to such phenomena as the facial tattoos of the Caduveo Indians. The complete analysis is too rich for any full description here; suffice it to say that he sees the design of these facial decorations, with their interplay of symmetry and dissymmetry, as a "complex situation corresponding to two contradictory forms of duality, which results in a compromise realized by a secondary opposition between the axis of the object and that of the figure it represents."[70] This opposition, which the visual style is able to overcome in its own mode and by its own specifically pictorial means, essentially reflects the tension in Caduveo society between a tripartite and a binary form of social organization, one which the Caduveos were unable to overcome: "since they were unable to come to consciousness of this contradiction and to live it, they began to dream it."[71] Art, along with mythic narrative, may thus be seen as a working out in formal terms of what a culture is unable to resolve concretely; or, in our present terminology, we may say that for this view art is a sign-system, an articulation on the level of the signifier, of a signified which is essentially felt to be an antinomy or a contradiction.

Such a view ought to lead us to reflect on the relationship between an "opposition" and a "contradiction"; and it ought

[70] *Tristes tropiques*, p. 199.   [71] *Ibid.*, p. 203.

to find its fulfillment in the description of the mechanism by which such contradictions are to be understood as generating the more conscious levels of discourse out of themselves. It is at such a description that Greimas' study of the "elementary structure of signification" aims. This is what we may term, in contrast to Lévi-Strauss' "culinary triangle," the "semantic rectangle," and it is designed to diagram the way in which, from any given starting point S, a whole complex of meaning possibilities, indeed a complete meaning system, may be derived.

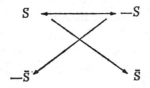

If, using Greimas' convenient example,[72] we take S to be the marriage rule of a given society, the semantic rectangle allows us to generate a complete table or inventory of the sexual conventions or possibilities of the society in question. So —S may be read as a symbol for those sexual relationships which are proscribed or considered abnormal (e.g., incest), while the simple negative S̄ stands for those relationships which are not matrimonial, i.e., not prescribed or legalized by the marriage system in force: these would be, for instance, adultery on the woman's part. The fourth term —S̄ may then be understood as the simple negative of the

[72] "Les Jeux des contraintes sémiotiques" (with François Rastier), in Du Sens, pp. 135-155, esp. pp. 141-144. (An English translation of this article has appeared in Yale French Studies, No. 41 [1968], pp. 86-105.) On the semantic rectangle, see also Vigo Brøndall, Essais de linguistique générale (Copenhagen, 1943), pp. 16-18 and 41-48; and Théorie des prépositions (Copenhagen, 1950), pp. 38-39; as well as Robert Blanché, Les Structures intellectuelles (Paris, 1966).

abnormal, forbidden relations, or in other words those sexual relationships which are neither abnormal nor explicitly forbidden: e.g., masculine adultery.

Greimas' rectangle is thus essentially an articulation of the traditional logical concepts of the contradictory and the contrary. Š is, we may say, a simple not-S, while —S must be thought of more strongly as a positive anti-S. In this sense, indeed, our starting point (the choice of the content of S) is in reality a binary opposition, for it is bound to include within itself a concept of its own anti-S, its own dialectical opposite. The codification of marriage law, in other words, implies a notion of the forbidden in its very structure. So the first merit of Greimas' mechanism is to enjoin upon us the obligation to articulate any apparently static free-standing concept or term into that binary opposition which it structurally presupposes and which forms the very basis for its intelligibility.

The next operation implicit in the mechanism might then be seen precisely as the unconscious meditation on the difference between the opposite of a given term (—S) and its simple negation (Š): in this sense to "articulate" the mechanism would mean repeatedly to try out one term after another, in order to measure the gap between them. Such articulation would thus be perfectly consistent with the narrative form as such, where the mind is confronted with a series of imaginative possibilities in succession. But it might also take the form of the invention of some mediatory concept which bridged the gap ("resolved" the insoluble contradiction). Or, finally, the mechanism may function as a kind of static value-system, in which raw material coming in from the outside (i.e., the necessities of a given plot) are at once given their place in the rectangular structure and transformed into symbolically signifying elements within the system. This is basically what Greimas shows to be at work in

Bernanos, whose semantic system he shows to be an articulation of the basic symbolic conflict between life and death. When, however, we replace this abstract structure with the concrete content of Bernanos' works, we discover the following pattern of relationships:[73]

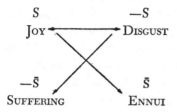

Yet insofar as Bernanos' characters and the events in his novels may be thought of as attempting in one way or another to bridge the gaps between these terms, we may speak of a number of complex formations or of possible mediations. Logically, the latter take the form of all the binary relationships possible between the four terms of the rectangle; yet we may particularly emphasize the concept of the "neuter," as a kind of neutralization of the initial opposition, the union of its two negations, one logically posterior to it, yet giving itself as the latter's zero degree or state of rest. In Bernanos this would no doubt take the form of some primal insensibility or indifference. For the other, primary side of the rectangle, literature and mythology know a host of mediatory figures, such as the trickster,[74] whose function is essentially to unite positive and negative, to solve or re-

[73] *Sémantique structurale*, p. 256.
[74] See *Anthropologie structurale*, pp. 247-251. Louis Marin's study of Judas, in *Sémiotique de la Passion*, is a remarkable analysis of the mechanisms of such mediations, and particularly of the role of neutralization and of the neuter in such an exchange. Thus, the Passion narrative involves a replacement of Jesus (the man, the name, the signifier) by God (the signified): "the traitor . . . operates this exchange through a neutralization of the signifier" (*op.cit.*, p. 140).

solve the opposition through their own complex personal characteristics or through the nimbleness of their actions. The imaginative vision is thus a kind of logical proof or demonstration in its own right: if the listener can visualize such a mediatory figure, then he has implicitly admitted the possibility of a concrete solution to his abstract dilemma.

In actual practice, however, it frequently turns out that we are able to articulate a given concept into only three of the four available positions; the final one, $-\bar{S}$, remains a cipher or an enigma for the mind. Thus Lévi-Strauss' well-known culinary triangle,[75] alluded to above, may very easily be reformulated along three of the four basic terms of our "elementary structure":

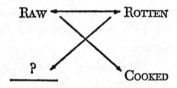

At this point, therefore, the development of the model may take two different directions. It may involve the replacement of the abstract terminology with a concrete content (smoked meat, boiled meat, roasted meat), which is thus valorized in a particular way by the basic system. Or it may take the form of a search for the missing term (FRESH), which we may now identify as none other than the "negation of a negation" familiar from dialectical philosophy. It is, indeed, because the negation of a negation is such a decisive leap, such a production or generation of new meaning, that we so frequently come upon a system in the incomplete state shown above (only three terms out of four given). Under such circumstances the negation of the

75 See *L'Origine des manières de table*, pp. 400-411.

negation then becomes the primary work which the mechanism is called upon to accomplish.

To give an example in the area of literary criticism, we may select Dickens' *Hard Times*, not only because it is familiar and relatively short, but also and primarily because, as Dickens' only didactic or "thesis" novel, it involves an idea content which has already been formulated for us by the author in terms of a binary opposition. In *Hard Times* we witness the confrontation of what amount to two antagonistic intellectual systems: Mr. Gradgrind's utilitarianism ("Facts! Facts!") and that world of anti-facts symbolized by Sissy Jupe and the circus, or in other words, imagination. The novel is primarily the education of the educator, the conversion of Mr. Gradgrind from his inhuman system to the opposing one. It is thus a series of lessons administered to Mr. Gradgrind, and we may sort these lessons into two groups and see them as the symbolic answers to two kinds of questions. It is as though the plot of the novel, seeking now to generate the terms $\bar{S}$ and $-\bar{S}$, were little more than a series of attempts to visualize the solutions to these riddles: What happens when you negate or deny imagination? What would happen if, on the contrary, you negated facts? Little by little the products of Mr. Gradgrind's system show us the various forms which the negation of the negation, which the denial of Imagination, may take: his son Tom (theft), his daughter Louisa (adultery, or at least projected adultery), his model pupil Blitzer (delation, and in general the death of the spirit). Thus the absent fourth term comes to the center of the stage; the plot is nothing but an attempt to give it imaginative being, to work through faulty solutions and unacceptable hypotheses until an adequate embodiment has been realized in terms of the narrative material.

167

THE STRUCTURALIST PROJECTION

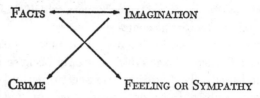

FACTS ←————→ IMAGINATION

CRIME   FEELING OR SYMPATHY

With this discovery (Mr. Gradgrind's education, Louisa's belated experience of family love), the semantic rectangle is completed and the novel comes to an end.

4

> Then we must admit, and not object to say, that motion is the same and is not the same, for we do not apply the terms "same" and "not the same" in the same sense; but we call it the "same" in relation to itself, because partaking of the same; and "not the same," because, having communion with the other, it is thereby severed from the same, and has not that but other, and is therefore rightly spoken of as "not the same."
>
> —Plato, *The Sophist.*

The previous sections taught the lesson that in the long run it is impossible to separate *signifié* from *signifiant* in any way that would be meaningful either methodologically or conceptually. With this realization, the third moment of Structuralism comes into being. This moment shifts its attention to the total sign itself, or rather to the process which creates it, and of which signifier and signified are themselves but moments, namely the process of signification. Now, indeed, the difficulty of keeping signifier and signified separate conceptually becomes a methodological advantage; for it is in that instant of separation, in that ephemeral void between the two which vanishes even as we stare at it, that signification itself as an emergence is to be found. Yet, inasmuch as the object is no longer a static one, to be studied in an external way, but rather a form of perception, an awareness of the interplay of the same and the other to be developed, the emphasis on signification takes the form of a mystery, the mystery of the incarnation of meaning in language, and as such its study is a kind of meditation. This is what accounts for the hermetic quality of the writers who deal with it. The sense of the esoteric may be understood, in Barthes' sense, precisely as a sign, as a way of signifying ritual and the presence of mystery, of underlining through the very temporal unfolding of the ritual language the sacred quality of the object itself. It is no accident that the style of Lacan suggests that of Mallarmé, that that of Derrida suggests Heidegger, both of whom expressed in the very movement of their periods the essential nature of the text as initiation.

1. Lacan's doctrine, embodied in oral seminars and taking as its very object the therapeutic process, is openly initiatory, and we cannot hope to give more than a feeling for its general direction. It consists, as we have already suggested, in a translation of the Freudian topology into linguistic terms, so that eventually all of the apparently experiential or even existential phenomena dealt with by Freud (desire, anxiety, the Oedipus complex, the death wish) will be reformulable in terms of the linguistic model.

The privileged position of psychoanalysis with respect to signification and its emergence may be measured by the fact that its object of study is not so much the things themselves—such as sexual desire in itself—but rather the process of coming into being of desire, or its failure to come into being. Thus the psychoanalytic understanding is already in its very nature a heightened awareness of identity and difference, of presence and absence, of that twilight in which a given type of signification is both there and not there yet.[76] We recall that for Lacan the acquisition of language by the

[76] This is the exemplary value of the cry of little Hans ("Fort! Da!"); see Wilden, *The Language of the Self*, p. 163 and passim.

infant (*infans*: speechless) marks his accession to the symbolic order; this fact of a genesis allows Lacan to oppose need to desire in much the same way that Lévi-Strauss opposes nature to culture, for the two are in a sense operational concepts only. Pure physical need has no more existence than the state of nature, and is at once transformed into desire on its passage through the field of the Symbolic, where it becomes invested with value of a social character, and in particular associated with the other in its various forms.

What complicates Lacan's view is that for him language is at one and the same time the *id* or unconscious out of which the subject emerges ("Wo *es* war, soll *Ich* werden" is the classic formula of Freud himself) and that symbolic realm into which he emerges as well, that set of coordinates in terms of which he finally determines his own place and function. Thus the Oedipus complex is ultimately resolved through recourse to what Lacan calls the "Name-of-the-Father," by which he means the subject's discovery that he does not want to be his father (essentially an *imaginary* ambition), but merely to assume his function or "name" in that *symbolic* realm in which fatherhood itself is defined and marked off as a particular role. The opposition of the Imaginary to the Symbolic may be understood as a distinction between the subject's investment of energy in his own image, on the one hand, and, on the other, his ultimate acceptance of the secondary status of consciousness with respect to the linguistic order itself.

As for the identification between language and the unconscious, it may perhaps best be approached through reference to Lacan's well-known programmatic slogan: "L'inconscient, c'est le discours de l'autre." This seems to me to be a sentence rather than an idea, by which I mean that it marks out the place of a meditation and offers itself as an object of exegesis, instead of serving as the expression of a single concept.[77] That the unconscious should be thought of as the discourse of the other at once places us before a set of terms which it is our task to recombine in all their possible permutations. In a very general way, we may say that the linguistic situation involves, not only an abstract category of otherness that precedes all empirical experience of the other, not only a concrete and empirical other person also, but, together with those two elements, yet a third, which is my own alter-ego, or my image of myself (derived ultimately from the mirror stage of infancy, when the child first learns that he possesses an external image). When we stop to consider that the other person's experience of language is also articulated into these various dimensions, we come little by little to realize that the act of speech is one which involves the most elaborate (imaginary) projections and cross-identifications, in which otherness itself opens up a privileged place for what we customarily call the unconscious.

What the form of Lacan's doctrine implies, however, is that these are things which must be lived rather than known abstractly. Indeed, the privileged position of the dream or of the witticism derives precisely from the fact that we can understand them only by re-assisting at the process of emergence which they constitute. So also, for instance, when one reviews the content of Lacan's seminars—such as the one spent in demonstrating the generation of a language system out of numbers or initial unities[78]—it is difficult to avoid the impression that, whatever the official value of consciousness or the cogito in this system, Lacanian training essentially involves a stimulation and articulation of the pre-conscious as an intuitive sense of Identity and Difference, or of what we have called the emergence of signification.

[77] For the ambiguity of the genitive in the sentence, for instance, see Lacan, *Écrits*, pp. 814-815.
[78] *Ibid.*, pp. 46-53.

So far, however, we have given only the relatively philosophical or epistemological dimension of this teaching. When we come now to what are felt to be the more characteristically Freudian phenomena, such as the neuroses and the etiology of desire, I may rashly hazard the following brief description of Lacan's system: the experience of the mother is one of an initial plenitude from which the infant is brusquely severed. Thus, the separation from the mother results in a kind of primal lack or *béance*, a "gaping," and it is this traumatic experience which is customarily felt (by both girls and boys) as a castration. Note that just as language is a kind of *béance* or opening onto the Other (it is never a plenitude itself, always in its very structure a formed incompleteness, waiting for the Other's participation), so also the phallus is to be understood as part of the realm of the Symbolic rather than as the penis itself. The phallus is thus a linguistic category, the very symbol of lost plenitude, and sexual desire, insofar as it is an attempt to regain that plenitude, to repossess the phallus, is also a ratification of its loss. This is to say that neurosis for Lacan is essentially a failure to accept castration, a failure to accept the primal lack which is at the center of life itself: a vain and impossible nostalgia for that first essential plenitude, a belief that one really can in one form or another repossess the phallus. Genuine desire on the other hand is a consent to incompleteness, to time and to the repetition of desire in time; whereas the disorders of desire result from an attempt to keep alive the delusion and the fiction of ultimate satisfaction. Lacan's stoicism is thus the antithesis of the sexual optimism of a Wilhelm Reich, whose doctrine of orgasm amounts to what the Structuralists would no doubt think of as a myth of total satisfaction, analogous to that myth of total presence denounced by Derrida: we will see shortly the kinship between this notion of neurosis as an attempt to achieve ultimate certainty, and Derrida's denunciation of the need for some ultimate, transcendental signified in the Western philosophical tradition. For the moment, I do not feel it would be playing on words too much to see in Lacanian castration a kind of zero degree of the psychic—that essential charged absence around which the entire meaning- or language-system necessarily organizes itself.

2. Derrida's special position in Structuralism is founded on the refusal of the initial problem raised in the previous section, that of the ultimate status of signified with respect to signifier or, in more common language, of the relationship between thoughts and words. Yet for Derrida the problem is useful in that, even though false, it is symptomatic of a profound disorder in Western philosophy as a whole. It is here that his work most closely follows Heidegger's critique of history, even though the terms in which he formulates his own ideas are not those—loss of the mystery of the *Seinsfrage* or of the meditation on being—in which Heidegger expresses himself. He also invokes Nietzsche, whose critique of transcendence and of Western metaphysics is not without resemblance to his own position. The very problem of a relationship between thoughts and words betrays a metaphysics of "presence," and implies an illusion that univocal substances exist, that a pure present exists, in which we come face to face once and for all with objects; that meanings exist, such that it ought to be possible to "decide" whether they are initially verbal or not; that there is such a thing as knowledge which one can acquire in some tangible or permanent way. All of these concepts are basically hypostases of the initial metaphysic of absolute presence which encourages the subject (in that not unlike the optical illusion of the Sartrean *en-soi*) in the belief that, no matter what his own fragmentary experience, somewhere absolute plenitude exists. It is this belief in presence which forms the *clôture* or

conceptual ceiling of Western thought; and Derrida's own dilemma lies in the fact that he is himself part of that tradition, inextricably involved in its language and institutions, and condemned to the impossible situation (which resembles Barthes' description of the impossibility of literature) of denouncing the metaphysic of presence with words and terminology which, no sooner used, themselves solidify and become instruments in the perpetuation of that illusion of presence which they were initially designed to dispel.

Hence the recourse to a kind of violence done to language by which Derrida (like Heidegger, and both of them following the Platonic example of etymological argumentation) attempts to hold open a special place within his words in such a way that his terminology cannot settle back down into the illusory order of nouns and substances. It is also the notion of difference or differance, by which Derrida means to stress the profound identity between what would in English be distinguished as to *differ* and to *defer*. Difference (which is, as we have seen, the very basis of linguistic structure itself, and is in a sense at one with the feeling of identity as well) is a differance or deferring in its essential temporality, its structure as sheer process, which can never be arrested into static presence; which, even as we become aware of it, glides beyond our reach in time, so that its presence is at one and the same instant an absence as well.

The form which this differance takes in language is called by Derrida the "trace." It is through the concept of the trace that Derrida annuls the false problem of words versus meanings which we evoked above. For to attempt to go back behind the sentence or the word that already exists, behind the thought that has already taken verbal form, is to submit to the prestige of a "myth of origins," and to attempt to re-place ourselves artificially in a past in which that living unity had not yet taken place, in which there still was such a thing as pure sound on the one hand, and pure meaning or idea on the other, as in some lumber room before the creation of the world. To say that all language is a *trace* is to underscore the paradox of signification: namely, that in order to be aware of it at all, it must already have happened; it is an event which is always in the past, even though in an immediate one. Thus we might invoke a sentence of Hegel of which the existentialists were also fond in their own way: "Wesen ist, was gewesen ist" (essence is what has already taken place), a formula by which Hegel translates the static categories of knowledge into profoundly historical and temporal phenomena in movement, and which in our present context we might render by saying, "Meaning is in its very structure always a *trace*, an already-happened."

The consequence of this idea is that the sign is always somehow impure. Our uncertainty before it, the ambiguous way in which it gives itself now as transparency and now as barrier, in which we are mentally able to alternate pure sound and pure meaning—all these things are not so much the result of our imperfect knowledge of the phenomenon in question but are rather founded in the very structure of language itself. To say that the sign is of necessity a trace is to admit that any sign can be focussed either materially or conceptually, that a sign both is and is not matter, and carries within itself a kind of necessary exteriority. In this sense, the myth of presence is at one with the myth of pure speech, or of the priority of the spoken over the written. In a series of analyses (Plato, Rousseau, Saussure, Husserl) Derrida shows how the instinctive privilege granted the oral can ultimately be traced back to an illusion of absolute transparency of meaning, or in other words absolute presence. His system thus stands as the reversal of everything valor-

175

ized by MacLuhanism; yet the great achievements of the latter movement—such as Walter J. Ong's *Presence of the Word*—confirm Derrida even to the identification between the evolution of writing and the stages of psychosexual development and may indeed be read in conjunction with him as two opposites which, speaking positively and negatively of the same level of cultural reality, find a profound identity.

It follows from this repudiation of the pretenses of the spoken word that for Derrida the essential structure of all language, even that of pre-literate or oral cultures, is essentially that of script: arch-script or *archi-écriture* as he terms it, in order to emphasize this essential exteriority or distance from itself which all language bears within itself and upon which all later, empirical writing-systems are founded. This means, for one thing, that there is always a gap between a text and its meaning, that commentaries or interpretations are generated out of an ontological lack with the text itself. But it also implies that a text can have no ultimate meaning, and that the process of interpretation, of unfolding the successive layers of the signified, each of which is then in its own turn transformed into a new signifier or signifying system in its own right, is properly an infinite one.

It is here that with the group around the review *Tel Quel* (founded in 1960) Derrida's metaphysical critique, which bears marked analogies with that of Heidegger and is indeed strongly influenced by the latter, acquires its political content. I am indeed tempted to characterize the *Tel Quel* circle as Left-Heideggerians (in allusion to the Left-Hegelians from whose atmosphere Marx himself emerged) on account of their identification of authoritarianism and theocentrism with the commitment to some Absolute Signified. Yet it is not too much to say that these writers, closely associated with the Communist Party, embody as radical and original a political conception as any since that of the Surrealist movement in the early thirties.

For Derrida's original vision of the explanatory force of the notion of script may be said to have left a place open for Marxism. Certainly it already included Freudianism to the degree to which Freudianism itself included a reflection on language and script. We have only to think of that Mystic Writing Pad which Freud evoked to convey a picture of the relationship of conscious to unconscious[79] to sense the degree to which analogies of writing saturate the psychoanalytic model. Such fluoroscopy of the text, philosophical or literary, such minute detection of the presence, either lexicological or syntactic, of the graphological analogy, may be said to constitute what is characteristic of Derrida's method, as opposed to his actual system itself. It is a canon which sees such figural content, even where apparently inconsequential, as privileged and symptomatic of the writer's relationship to script, or in other words of his practice of the myth of presence within the conceptual framework of the tradition of Western metaphysics. We may give as an example of the possibilities of such analysis the terms in which Gide's "immoralist," reborn to life, designates his rediscovery of the " 'old Adam' whom the Gospels wanted to do away with; whom everything around me, books, teachers, family and even I myself had attempted to suppress. And as wasted as he was, and difficult to distinguish beneath so many overprints [*surcharges*], it seemed to me all the more essential and meritorious to rediscover him. From then on I despised that secondary habitual being which education had drawn [*dessiné*] over on top of him. I had to shake off those layers of super-impressions.

"And I compared myself to palimpsests; I knew the schol-

[79] "A Note on the 'Mystic Writing-Pad' " (1925), in Sigmund Freud, *General Psychological Theory* (New York, 1963), pp. 207-212.

ar's joy, who discovers an older and infinitely more precious text beneath more recent lines upon the same paper. What was that hidden secret text? And would it not be necessary to erase the more recent ones in order to read it?"[80]

L'Immoraliste thus becomes the story of a textual decipherment: its emblematic landscapes, the oases and the lush Norman farm, are so many forms of a visible script, in which nature in the guise of spring or annual rainfall, and culture, in the methods of cultivating the soil, combine to write the calligraphy of man himself. Nor are the other dimensions of such analysis so very far away either; for the book is quite deliberately a reflection on the antinomies of private property and ownership on the one hand, while the theme of homosexuality may be said to be motivated by the very image of the palimpsest itself, to the degree to which that deepest layer of script—"a kind of stubborn perseverance in the worst"[81]—must of necessity be *different* from the higher ones in order to be distinguishable from them in the first place. Vice, said Sartre once, is a taste for failure; and it is in Gide (think of the situation in which Michel ends up helping the poachers steal from *himself*) the penalty for an allegiance to the myth of some absolute and original presence.

It should be observed that such a method (faithful in that, indeed, to the structure of Gide's fable) is essentially allegorical in nature. The reader of Derrida's own analyses cannot fail to be struck by the way in which they so often seem to revert to the oldest forms of Freudian interpretation, to so-called phallic symbolism. Thus in his study of the early "Project for a Scientific Psychology" of Freud himself,[82]

---

[80] André Gide, *L'Immoraliste* (Paris, 1929), pp. 61-62.
[81] *Ibid.*, p. 171.
[82] In "Freud et la scène de l'écriture," Jacques Derrida, *L'Écriture et la différence* (Paris, 1967), pp. 293-340.

Derrida interprets the word "Bahnung" ("frayage" or "piercing through," most imperfectly translated as "facilitation" in the Standard Edition), a term designed to underscore economic relationships between various parts of the psyche, as a twin image of the act of inscribing a text and of sexual penetration: so Freud (who was well aware of the sexual symbolism of writing "which consists of releasing liquid from a pen onto blank paper")[83] is used against himself. The most completely worked out example of such a symbolic correlation of writing and sexuality is however given in Derrida's *De la grammatologie*, where Rousseau's description of script as a mere "supplement" to spoken language is shown to conceal an unconscious identification between writing and masturbation (also described by Rousseau as a "supplement" in the sense of a substitute or a replacement of nature).

To describe such analysis as allegorical is not to claim that it is false. Indeed the analysis of Rousseau is most convincing in this respect and finds confirmation in an independent study of Rousseau's own psychology on the one hand, and in the more general status of literature in the eighteenth century as an essentially titillating or pornographic representation on the other. Yet it would be a mistake—although not incorrect either—to defend Derrida's method on the grounds of some process of idea-association according to which a given term (Rousseau's *supplément*, Plato's *pharmakon*) attracts a symbolic investment of all kinds of essential content and may therefore serve as a kind of symptom for the exploration of the work as a whole. Rather, the key word, insofar as it is a sign, includes within itself a fundamental gap—or *différence*, or *différance*—between the signifier and the signified, such that we are never

---

[83] Quoted in Derrida, *L'Écriture et la différence*, p. 338.

179

able to attain its "ultimate" meaning, that meaning which would be able to be pure presence or identity with itself. Thus the very structure of the sign is allegorical, in that it is a perpetual movement from one "level" of the signified to another from which it is expulsed in its turn in infinite regression.

It is in this context that the *Tel Quel* group may be said, not to appropriate, but to bring to completion, Derrida's essential concept. Indeed, the monument to their collective efforts, Jean-Joseph Goux's *Numismatiques*, resembles nothing quite so much as a return to the all-encompassing architectonics of the patristic and medieval system of the four levels of interpretation. For Goux aims here at demonstrating the basic identity of value systems in general, whether on the economic, psychoanalytic, political, and linguistic levels: how "a *hierarchy* (of values) is established. A principle of order and of subordination according to which the great (complex and multiform) majority of 'signs' (products, acts and gestures, subjects, objects) are ranged beneath the *sacred authority* of certain of their number. At certain points of condensation value seems to be stored up, capitalized, centralized, investing given elements with some privileged representativity, indeed even with the *monopoly of representativity* within that diversified collection of which they are themselves elements. Promotion whose enigmatic genesis is then effaced, making their monopoly absolute (detached and unlimited) in their transcendental role as a *standard* and a *measure* of values."[84]

The rich analogical content of the various local studies of value—Marx's analysis of money and the commodity, Freud's of the libido, Nietzsche's of ethics, Derrida's of the

[84] Jean-Joseph Goux, "Numismatiques," 2 Parts (*Tel Quel*, No. 35, Fall, 1968, pp. 64-89, and No. 36, Winter, 1968, pp. 54-74), Part I, p. 65.

word—is itself a sign of the hidden interrelationships of the categories which govern these various dimensions: gold, the phallus, the father or the monarch or God, and the myth of the *parole pleine* or spoken word. The paradigm for the genesis of these absolute standards is Marx's description of the four stages of the exchange mechanism: simple (the moment of a one-to-one relationship, equated with Lacan's mirror stage), developed (a kind of polymorphous value system), generalized (in which the abstract idea of a common value emerges), and finally monetary or absolute (where gold is removed from the commodity circuit and made the absolute standard, just as the father is killed and then transformed into the Name-of-the-Father, just as, for Lacanian psychoanalysis, symbolic castration fixates sexuality at the genital stage). The other basic moment of the process—and it is this which confers a political and revolutionary content on the demonstration—is the effacement or occultation of the evolutionary process itself, whereby the bourgeoisie conceals from itself the source of value in genuine labor, banishes the other moments of the sexual evolution to the limbo of perversion, destroys all traces of the murder of the father, assimilates all script-like manifestations of language to mere "supplements" of the spoken word itself.

The political ethic—implicit in Derrida, outspoken in the *Tel Quel* group—thus manifests itself as "the struggle against *the hypostatized result of a genesis effaced*";[85] and to express it this way is to understand the value as well as the limits of this position within the Marxist framework. I have distinguished elsewhere[86] between a vulgar-Marxist use of economic homologies—an essentially allegorical translation into Marxist economic terminology—and that more

[85] "Numismatiques," Part II (*Tel Quel*, No. 36), p. 74.
[86] See my *Marxism and Form*, pp. 375-381.

genuinely revolutionary gesture which seeks to reground thought in the concrete situation of class struggle. The politics of *Tel Quel* may in such a context essentially be defined as a militant atheism which struggles against the notion, on all levels, of a transcendental signifier or ultimate substantialized dimension of meaning or absolute presence. It may be seen as a continuation of the enterprise of the Sartre of *Being and Nothingness*, except that now the very term and category of being itself has been repudiated, and in place of the relatively static perseverance in not-being which was the ethical conclusion of Sartre's work, *Tel Quel* foresees a kind of consent to time or process, to a kind of total textual productivity or production of the *trace* which would be that of reality itself. Julia Kristeva has given the most systematic expression to these ideas in the literary realm, proposing to replace the older metaphysical notions of literary form with that of the text as a self-generating mechanism, as a perpetual process of textual *production*.

The repression of such productivity would then result from a fear of the process of infinite regression described above, that infinite relay of meaning from signifier to signified; the bourgeois or neurotic (Sartre's *salauds*) is unable to live within this pure temporality of differance and must ultimately have recourse to some comforting doctrine of a transcendental signified at whatever level, whether it be that of God, political authority, *machismo*, the literary work, or simply meaning itself. Thus, with the *Tel Quel* group, the scattered implications of Lacan and Derrida come together with a force which, if it is not ultimately revolutionary, is at least explosively critical within the bourgeois tradition.

At the same time, it must be observed that the system on which it is based is ultimately self-contradictory. In the very act of repudiating any ultimate or transcendental signified, any concept which would dictate the ultimate or fundamental content of reality, Derrida has ended up inventing a new one, namely that of script itself. In literary terms, we may say that Derrida's own analyses—not to speak of the polyphony of Goux's elaboration—depend for their force on the isolation and valorization of script as a unique and privileged type of content: script has thus become the basic interpretive or explanatory code, one which is felt to have a priority over the other types of content (economic, sexual, and political) which it orders beneath itself in the hierarchy of the interpretive act. One cannot otherwise account for the force of a passage such as the following one, quite characteristic of Derrida's argumentation: "Script, letter, sensible inscription have always been considered in the Western tradition as body and matter external to spirit, to breath, to the Word and to Logos. And the problem of the soul and the body is *doubtless* derived from the problem of script to which it *seems*—inversely—to lend its own metaphors."[87] The reversal is disingenuous to the degree that it offers a simple choice of options; for it is only too clear that if the mind-body problem is privileged, then the whole notion of trace and differance may be seen as little more than one manifestation among others (this one on the linguistic level) of some basic necessity for life to be embodied or physically incarnated. We are here asked to choose between two ways of expressing the same thing, two analogous codes or explanatory systems—that of language and that of life or organism; at this particular stage, the choice looks suspiciously like a metaphysical option, and Derrida's notion of the trace suspiciously like yet another ontological theory of the type it was initially designed to denounce.

I do not, however, want to imply that his system is wholly

[87] Jacques Derrida, *De la grammatologie* (Paris, 1967), p. 52, italics mine.

irreconcilable with Marxism. Indeed, in its emphasis on the paradoxical structure of the present or of consciousness, always already in place and in situation, always somehow preceding themselves in time and being, Derrida's thought here rejoins Althusser's notion of the "toujours-déjà-donné": "In the place of the ideological myth of a philosophy of origins and its organic concepts, Marxism establishes as its guiding principle the recognition of the givenness of the complex structure of every concrete 'object,' a structure which governs both the development of the object itself and the development of that theoretical praxis which produces knowledge of the object. We thus no longer have to do with some original essence, but with something always given in advance [*un toujours-déjà-donné*], no matter how far back into the past knowledge may go."[88] In this context, the "trace" thus becomes a striking, symbolic way of conveying Marx's ever-scandalous discovery that "it is not the consciousness of men that determines their existence, but on the contrary their social existence determines their consciousness."[89] This determination makes itself felt in the "déjà-donné," which always transcends consciousnsss as a given, no matter how exhaustively it is assumed, just as it finds its visual representation in the geological deposits of language as script. Such a dimension might well be seen as the ultimate bedrock of the signified—that level of the infrastructure or of "social being" which never comes to formulation as a concept or signifier in its own right, which is therefore never accessible to the kind of unconscious theological fixation which has been described above, yet which places a floor beneath the infinite regression and flight of the signifier. But if this is the case, then the hypostases denounced by

[88] Althusser, *Pour Marx*, pp. 203-204.
[89] Marx and Engels, *Basic Writings on Politics and Philosophy*, ed. L. S. Feuer (New York, 1959), p. 43.

Derrida ought more properly to be thought of as transcendental *signifiers*, in that they amount to a fixation on a single type of sign or conceptual category. The ultimate dimension of the signified to which we have alluded cannot, however, be hypostasized in this way (the economism of vulgar Marxism is an attempt to do so), since it is always beyond individual consciousness and is rather that ultimate ground from which individual consciousness arises.

The dilemma is itself, however, but the reflection of the starting point of Structuralism, already evoked in the preface: to choose to speak of reality in terms of linguistic systems, to re-express the problems of philosophy in the new linguistic terminology, is of necessity an arbitrary and absolute decision, one which makes of language itself a privileged mode of explanation. To appeal to the growing use of the linguistic model by contemporaries and predecessors alike is to have recourse to the *Zeitgeist*, if not to changes in fashion; and it seems more honest to admit that the notion that everything is language is as indefensible as it is unanswerable.

Derrida knows this so well that he is led to the ultimate conclusion that Structuralism itself suffers under the spell of a myth of presence: "The foundations of the metaphysic of presence have been shaken by means of the concept of a *sign*. But as soon as one attempts to show . . . that there is no transcendental or privileged signified and that at that point the field or play of signification knows no limit, then one ought—but this is exactly what one cannot do—to refuse the very concept and word sign. For the signification 'sign' has always been understood and determined in its meaning as a sign-of, as a signifier pointing back to, a signified, as a signifier different from its signified. If now we erase the radical difference between signifier and signified, then we ought to abandon the very word signifier itself as

185

involving an essentially metaphysical concept. When Lévi-Strauss, in his preface to *Le Cru et le cuit*, says that he 'has attempted to transcend the opposition between the sensory and the intelligible by immediately installing [himself] on the level of signs,' the necessity, the force, and the legitimacy of his gesture cannot allow us to overlook the fact that the concept of the sign cannot in itself transcend this opposition between the sensory and the intelligible. It is itself determined by that opposition, utterly and completely and throughout its entire history. Its vitality derives precisely from that opposition and from the system which the latter sets up. Yet we cannot do without the concept of sign, we cannot renounce the metaphysical complicity involved in it without at the same moment renouncing the very work of criticism which we are directing against it, without running the risk of erasing the difference in the inner identity of a signified which has absorbed its signifier into itself, or, what amounts to the same thing, has completely exteriorized it."[90]

Thus Derrida's thought denies itself the facile illusion of having passed beyond the metaphysics of which it stands as a critique; of having emerged from the old models into some unexplored country whose existence such a critique had implied, if only by the negation of a negation. Instead, his philosophic language feels its way gropingly along the walls of its own conceptual prison, describing it from the inside as though it were only one of the possible worlds of which the others are nonetheless inconceivable.

5

1. This final moment of Structuralism, or of the Structuralist critique of Structuralism, allowed us to witness the

[90] *L'Écriture et la différence*, pp. 412-413.

destructive effect, within the static concept of the sign, of the fact and experience of temporality itself, which little by little comes to split open the husk of the older system and to budge visibly before the naked eye. One is tempted to speak here of a Structuralist reinvention of history, and, indeed, it seems to me that the word "differance" attempts to name the smallest differential event, to search out the mystery of time within its tiniest seeds. Derrida is well aware of this, and if he hesitates to use the word "historical" to describe the basic process involved, it is because for him Hegel is a metaphysician, and "history" (as an illusion of linear succession, of idealistic continuity, of a series of "presences") remains part of the metaphysical apparatus of the Western tradition: "If the word 'history' did not itself include the motivation of an ultimate repression of difference, one could say that only differences can be from the outset completely 'historical' in nature."[91]

This reinvention is at one with a profound reorganization of our habitual concepts of time and in particular, as might be expected from Derrida's terminology, with a thoroughgoing critique of the idea of a present. In some way yet to be determined, a genuine historicity is possible only on condition this illusion of an absolute present can be done away with, and the present opened up again to the drift from the other ends of time. This is, once again, why the work of art is in this context a privileged object of study: "This historicity of the work lies not only in the *past* of the work, in that sleep or vigil by which it precedes itself in the very intention of its author, but also in its impossibility of ever existing in the *present*, of being resumed in whatever absolute simultaneity or instantaneity."[92] Thus a new and profoundly

[91] Jacques Derrida, "La Différance," in *Tel Quel: Théorie d'ensemble*, p. 50.
[92] *L'Écriture et la différence*, p. 26.

historical awareness of time is the ultimate form taken by the Saussurean play of Identity and Difference: presence and absence in the moment itself, the generation of time out of stillness before our very eyes.

With this, Structuralism touches its outside limit, and it is worth pointing out that temporality here has become visible in Structuralist terms only because it is the temporality latent within the sign itself, and not the temporality of the object, not that of lived existence on the one hand, or of history on the other.

This separation is maintained in the most completely worked out statement of the Structuralist position on history, that of Althusser, for whom, as we have shown already, the conceptual world is to be held completely apart from the real: thus the problem of the concept of history is essentially a question of models, and not of realities. "We should have no illusions as to the incredible force of that prejudice, which still dominates us all, which is the very essence of contemporary historicity, and which attempts to make us confuse the object of knowledge with the real object, by affecting the object of knowledge with the very 'qualities' of the real object of which it is knowledge. The knowledge of history is no more historical than the knowledge of sugar is sweet."[93]

This is what Greimas has emphasized in a somewhat different way[94] when he reminds us that understanding is essentially a synchronic process, even when it takes diachronic events as its object. It follows that insofar as we can "apprehend" history at all conceptually, such apprehension must have taken the form of a translation of genuine diachrony into synchronic terms. Real diachrony, therefore, real his-

[93] *Lire le Capital*, I, p. 132.
[94] See "Structure et histoire," in Greimas, *Du Sens*, pp. 103-115.

tory, falls outside the mind as a kind of *Ding-an-sich,* unattainable directly: time becomes an unknowable.

Althusser's position is similar, although he is perhaps more consistent terminologically when he points out that both diachrony and synchrony are conceptual categories and that it is "lived" history (the experience of the individual) and "objective" history (the unfolding of collective destinies) which are the unknowables. Diachrony, as a mode of thought, thus becomes for him "a time of time, a complex time that one cannot *read* in the continuity of the time of life or of clocks, but that one must *construct* out of the specific structures of production itself"[95]—in other words a set of fictive or hypothetical models of change. This is also true of synchrony as well, which is for Althusser an abstraction from the richness of the contemporary, of a complex "structure à dominante," in which various levels of phenomenon are ordered hierarchically with respect to each other.

Thus Althusser's position constitutes an attack on both the empirical or realist and the Hegelian or idealist concepts of history, which he assimilates to each other as two dialectical opposites: "Here we are at the very antipodes of visible empirical history, where the time of all histories is the simple time of continuity, and where the 'contents' are simply the empty shape of the events which take place in it, which the historian then attempts to order with various editing techniques in order to 'periodize' this continuity. Instead of these categories of the continuous and discontinuous which make up the flat mystery of ordinary history, we have to deal with infinitely more complex categories, specific to each type of history, where there intervene new logical forms, where to be sure the Hegelian schemes, which are but the

[95] *Lire le Capital,* Vol. i, pp. 125-126.

sublimation of categories of the 'logic of movement and time,' have nothing but a highly approximative value, and even that only on condition of making an approximative (indicative) use of them corresponding to their approximation —for if we had to take these Hegelian categories for adequate ones, their use would then become theoretically absurd, and practically vain or catastrophic."[96]

2. It would seem that we have reached a reversal of positions which is itself profoundly dialectical in nature. For at this point, history seems to have become so deeply convinced of its own historical nature that it transcends itself qua history, and suddenly becomes the object of a non-historical type of knowledge. This is what has already happened in a relatively external way in the work of Lévi-Strauss, for whom the identification of history with modern or Western ("hot") society involves a consequent identification of primitive or cold societies with the a-historical, and the need to posit some wider third term (structure) which can subsume both. This is to confuse or at the very least to identify history as historical thinking, with history as the dynamic built-in principle of historical change within society itself. The result is that, on the one hand, the emergence of history (that is to say, the West) becomes for Lévi-Strauss something profoundly accidental, something which need never have taken place,[97] and, on the other,

[96] *Ibid.*, p. 129.

[97] "For if myths originating in the most backward cultures of the New World immediately place us on that decisive level of human consciousness which in our own culture marks the accession, first to philosophy and then to science, when nothing of that sort happened in the other, primitive culture, then one must conclude from this discrepancy that the transformation was necessary neither here nor there, and that states of thought which are meshed in together with each other do not succeed each other spontaneously or by some ineluctable causality." Claude Lévi-Strauss, *Du miel dans les cendres*, p. 408.

actual change is associated with objects rather than human action, and history becomes the history of things: "the difference [between mythical and logical thinking] has less to do with the quality of the intellectual operations involved than with the nature of the things on which those operations are directed. Technological specialists have long been aware of this in their own domain: an iron axe is not superior to a stone axe because one is 'better made' than the other. Both are equally well made, but iron is simply not the same as stone."[98] Lévi-Strauss' identification with Rousseau is thus the mark of a surprising identity in their basic philosophical positions.

But it is the work of Michel Foucault which is perhaps the most symptomatic of this process in which "history" becomes merely one form of mind among many other equally privileged forms. His book *Les Mots et les choses* has indeed the added interest for us of being an explicit attempt to work out the kind of history of models which, as we have already seen, the Structuralist position seemed to promise.

The critical concept which occupies much the same place in Foucault's analyses as does the idea of a "metaphysic of presence" in Derrida's is that of representation, or in other words a conception of the relationship of idea to object or word to thing in which the former would stand in one way or another as a mimesis of the latter. Foucault's purpose is to demonstrate "the coherence which existed throughout the classical period [by this, of course, is meant the 17th and 18th centuries] between the theory of representation and those of language, the natural orders, and riches and value. It is this configuration which at the beginning of the nineteenth century changes completely; the theory of representation disappears as a general foundation for all possible or-

[98] Lévi-Strauss, *Anthropologie structurale*, p. 255.

ders; language as a spontaneous tableau and first graphic ordering out of things, as an indispensable relay between representation and the things themselves, is now in its turn effaced; a profound historicity penetrates to the very heart of things, isolates them and defines them in their own coherence, imposes on them forms of order which are implied by the continuity of time; the analysis of exchange and currency makes way for the study of production, that of the organism takes precedence over an examination of taxonomic characteristics; and above all language loses its privileged position and becomes in its turn just one more figure of a history coherent with the very density of its own past. But as things little by little become centered on themselves, seeking the principle of their intelligibility in their development alone and abandoning the space of representation, man in his turn appears, for the first time in the history of Western knowledge. . . . From this are born all the chimeras of new humanisms, all the facile solutions of an 'anthropology' understood as a general, half-positivistic, half-philosophical reflection on man. It is comforting, however, and a profound appeasement, to think that man is but a recent invention, a figure not two centuries old, a simple fold in our knowledge, and that he will disappear when the latter has found a new form."[99]

We may summarize this new theory of history by following the destiny attributed in it to language, which is the guiding thread of the analysis: from the Renaissance (in which the world is essentially God's book, script, text, hieroglyph), through the classical period (with its dominant identification of grammar and logic), to modern times (with their essentially historical or genetic linguistics). History is thus marked by a gradual effacement of discourse, and now,

[99] Michel Foucault, *Les Mots et les choses* (Paris, 1966), pp. 14-15.

with the emergence of Structuralism, seems on the point of returning to a notion of the predominance of language (or of the Symbolic Order in general) over history or the cogito as outmoded forms of thought.

The paradigm is familiar enough, and indeed the interest of this particular work is perhaps proportionate to the unfamiliarity of the materials used as illustrations (linguistics, biology, economics). Foucault's earlier book, *Folie et Déraison*, less programmatic, was nonetheless more striking in the very project of a history of madness which it proposed. Yet the key "moments" were the same: the medieval, in which madmen wandered Europe free like gypsies, travelling the waterways on genuine "ships of fools," in which the "fool" was thought to possess divine privileges and wisdom (as still in Shakespeare); the classical, in which the emergent idea of reason generated its own dark opposite, and in which the first asylums, where for the first time madmen are shut away from the eye of the world, are contemporaneous with the Cartesian cogito; the romantic, where at Charenton madmen become the recipients of nineteenth-century philanthropy and insanity comes to be thought of, not as a crime, but as a disease; finally, our own time, where the great madmen, Nietzsche or Hölderlin or Antonin Artaud, are felt somehow to embody absolute experience, to possess the secrets of the limits of the personality and of the mind, indeed of reality itself.

The methodological problem that emerges starkly from these two works is not so much related to the content of the moments described, but rather to the passage from one moment to another. The very imagery with which Foucault describes this radical discontinuity between one moment and the next (earthquake, profound upheaval, seismographic rupture) constitutes a ratification, rather than a solution,

193

of the dilemma: "Perhaps it is not yet time to pose the problem: we must in all probability wait for the archeology of thought to be more solidly founded, for it to have more thoroughly taken the measure of what it is capable of describing directly and positively, for it to have described the singular systems and internal links to which it addresses itself, before it undertakes to walk around thought from the outside and question it on the direction in which it escapes itself. For the moment, let it suffice to receive these discontinuities in the empirical order, both obvious and obscure, in which they offer themselves."[100] Yet a theory of models ought to be in a privileged position to understand that the form of the model is in no way modified by the amount of empirical data available to it.

What has happened is that here, somehow, the incapacity of the doctrine of Identity and Difference to do anything other than register pure differences has come to the surface, and we have to do with an extreme version of the idea of the mutation, as a radical and meaningless shift from one internally coherent synchronic moment to another. But now Foucault's framework puts us in a position to see why this should be so: one cannot, in other words, reduce history to one form of understanding among others, and then expect to understand the links between those forms historically. One is reminded of Ponge's description of the trees, which try over and over to escape their treeness and end up simply producing more leaves: "On ne sort pas des arbres par des moyens d'arbre." All that Language as a transcendental signified can do is to understand history as one particular mode of discourse, and it remains gaping with amazement before a succession of forms which history itself understands simply as the life cycle of capitalism, from mercantile to post-industrial stages.

[100] *Ibid.*, pp. 64-65.

6

1. We have suggested that Structuralism can best be grasped as a philosophical formalism, as the extreme point of that general movement everywhere in modern philosophy away from positive content, and from the various dogmatisms of the signifier. Even the ambiguous positions of Freud and Marx in the Structuralist pantheon are clarified by this way of understanding its basic tendency; for both follow the end of systematic Western philosophy after Hegel, and both can be understood alternately as new *methods*, or new types of *content*: historical materialism and the psychoanalytic hermeneutic on the one hand, or dialectical materialism and the theory of the libido on the other. Structuralism has attempted, as we have seen, to assimilate these two methods, which it reads as twin versions of the gap between signifier and signified, while it has tended either to ignore the specific content of the two systems, or else to interpret it allegorically.

The drive towards formalism can be seen at work symptomatically in yet another way in Roland Barthes' distinction between a literary science and a literary criticism, a kind of reworking of the older distinction of Frege and Carnap between the *Sinn* and the *Bedeutung* of a given enunciation: its unchanging formal organization and that significance or changing evaluation to which it is put by successive generations of readers. The work would therefore be an equation whose variables we are free to fill in with whatever content or interpretive code we choose.[101] It is certain that Barthes has himself been faithful to this prescription, whose critical practice offers a variety of different critical codes, now explanation by trauma, now the Freudianism of *Totem and Taboo*, now that of Lacan, now the script-oriented in-

[101] See *Critique et et vérité*, esp. p. 56, as well as "Histoire ou littérature," in *Sur Racine*, pp. 145-167.

terpretations of *Tel Quel*. Yet these alternatives, while indicating the virtuosity of the interpreter, point to some basic structural flaw, some almost allegorical slackness, in the concept of the method itself, for which the refusal of all privileged content amounts to a license to use any kind indifferently.

At the same time, Structuralism, like the other great modern formalisms (pragmatism, phenomenology, logical positivism, existentialism) has helped to articulate the sense of this repugnance before content as such, by the nature of the particular type of content which it negates. In the case of Structuralism the privileged form of error is the idea of the substantialism of the ego or of the subject. Insofar as it has attempted to redissolve the subject into sheer relationality, into the systems of language or the Symbolic, Structuralism may be understood as a distorted awareness of the dawning collective character of life, as a kind of blurred reflection of the already collective structure of what is perhaps less the cybernetic than the mass-production commercial network into which our individual existences are organized. In this sense, the attack on the ego and on its pretensions is clearly an anti-idealistic impulse; it is, however, doubled with the relatively positivistic claim for the creation of a new type of objective science or semiology. Yet these positivistic elements—such as the hope of locating in the structure of the brain itself the source of the binary opposition—are less revealing than other structural consequences of the system of which we have now to speak.

Let us return to our long-suspended presentation of the analysis which Lévi-Strauss gives of the Oedipus myth. It will be recalled that the four basic types of episodes (incest, family murder, deformity, monsters) were there grouped into two pairs of oppositions, the one involving kinship relations (overestimation, underestimation), the other dealing with man's relationship to nature (from which he alternately succeeds and fails in freeing himself). In another section, moreover, we showed that for Lévi-Strauss a myth is essentially a means of resolving a real contradiction in the imaginary mode. Thus the Oedipus myth comes to be seen as a meditation on the contradiction between the kinship system on the one hand and nature on the other, a conceptually scandalized reaction to the failure of organic life to be wholly subsumed and absorbed by the pattern of the kinship rules and arrangements, which may be thought of as a kind of artistic sublimation and decoration of the purely animalic, on the order of facial tatoos. The myth "would then express the impossibility, for a society that professed to believe in the autochthony of man . . . to pass from this theory to the recognition of the fact that each one of us really is born of the union of a man and a woman. The difficulty is insurmountable. But the Oedipus myth offers a kind of instrumental logic which builds a bridge from the initial problem—is one born of one or two?—to the derived problem, which we may approximatively formulate as follows: is the same born from the same or the other? In this manner a correlation slowly disengages itself: the overestimation of kinship is to its underestimation as the attempt to escape autochthony is to the impossibility of doing so."[102]

The interpretation is an ingenious one, but it is far more than a local solution to one particular empirical mythological problem. For essentially the opposition described above is that of Nature to Culture; and insofar as the Oedipus myth involves a meditation by culture itself on its own origins, insofar as myth-making is not just an accidental but a constitutive part of culture itself, the myth as here inter-

[102] *Anthropologie structurale*, p. 239.

preted includes a reference to its own existence as well. Thus ultimately, for Lévi-Strauss, the interpretation of this particular myth (like that of all others) reveals "the distinctive character of myths which is, precisely, exaggeration, resulting from the multiplication of one level by another or by several others, and which, as in language itself, has as its function to signify signification. . . . And should it be asked to what ultimate signified these significations—which all signify each other but which ultimately have to relate to something—refer, then the only answer which this book [*Le Cru et le cuit*] has to offer is that myths *signify the spirit which elaborates them* by means of the world of which it is itself a part."[103] At this point, therefore, that double-functionality which formed the basis of Barthes' work (the sign both means something and points to its own existence as a sign) is here simplified into a thoroughgoing formalism in which the "content" is precisely the form itself: myths are *about* the mythological process, just like poems about poetry or novels about novelists. Only in this way can Lévi-Strauss avoid introducing extraneous content, a foreign body of imported and external "meaning," into these pure relational equations which are his structural analyses of myths: only thus can he avoid interpreting, but the way he does so ultimately has the result of turning the form of Structuralism (the linguistic model) into a new type of content (language as the ultimate signified).

That this is not merely a personal deviation, but rather a necessary structural distortion of the system as a whole, may be judged by another illustration drawn from literary criticism. For we have not yet touched on what is most distinctively Structuralist in the new literary criticism, whose plot-equations seemed continuations of research begun by the Formalists themselves. The most characteristic fea-

[103] *Le Cru et le cuit*, p. 346, italics mine.

ture of Structuralist criticism lies precisely in a kind of transformation of form into content, in which the form of Structuralist research (stories are organized like sentences, like linguistic enunciations) turns into a proposition about content: literary works are about language, take the process of speech itself as their essential subject matter. Thus in a series of striking articles Todorov shows that the very subject of such story-collections as the *Thousand and One Nights* must be seen as the act of storytelling itself, that the only constant of the psychology of the characters (or of the psychological presuppositions on which the work is founded) lies in the obsession with telling and listening to stories: what defines a character as a compositional unit is the fact of having a story to tell, and from the point of view of their ultimate destinies, "narration equals life: the absence of narration, death."[104] In much the same way, when we turn to a primitive epic like the *Odyssey*, and if the concept of speech is enlarged to include not only narration, but also supplication, boasting, the sirens' song, the lie (Cyclops' episode), little by little almost everything in the poem comes to seem a foregrounding of the act of speech itself, of the event of the word. Prophecy is particularly significant in this respect, for insofar as it redoubles everything that will actually happen, it causes us to see in events, not their existential immediacy, but a mere confirmation of speech itself, as events-already-narrated: "everything is told in advance; and everything which is told happens."[105]

When we turn now to a more complex literary form such as *Les Liaisons dangereuses*, we find analogous structures to be present: the epistolary novel proves to swarm with indications of all kinds, which for the most part take the

[104] Todorov, "Les Hommes-récits," in *Grammaire du Décaméron*, p. 92.
[105] Todorov, *Poétique de la prose* (Paris, 1971), p. 77.

form of a minute shift from the referential to the literal, in which the letter writer calls our attention to his own activity or to the words of his correspondent, to the *fact* of writing itself. The effects of writing and reading are thus promoted to the status of events within the novel, and end up displacing the "real" events which the letters were supposed to relate.

Yet from this undoubted structural peculiarity Todorov draws global conclusions which are symptomatic of structural interpretation generally: "Laclos thus symbolizes a profound quality of literature: the ultimate meaning of the *Liaisons dangereuses* is a proposition about literature itself. Every work, every novel, tells through its fabric of events the story of its own creation, its own history. Works such as those of Laclos or Proust only render explicit this truth which underlies all literary creation. Thus the vanity of all attempts to reach the ultimate meaning of a given novel or play becomes clear; the meaning of a work lies in its telling itself, its speaking of its own existence. Thus the novel tends to bring us before its own presence; and we can say that it begins where in fact it ends; for the very existence of the novel is the last link in its intrigue, and there where the narrated story, the story of life, ends, at exactly that point the narrating story, the story of literature, begins."[106] We have here to do, in short, with a reduplication on the level of structural analysis with that same return of the form upon itself, that same paradoxical self-designation which we watched taking place in Formalist criticism: where the latter saw the coming into existence of the work as the latter's ultimate content, now the Structuralists read the content of a given work as Language itself, and this is no mere accident or idiosyncrasy on the part of the individual

[106] Todorov, *Littérature et signification* (Paris, 1967), p. 49.

critic but rather a formal distortion inherent in the model itself.

So it is that we have found the practice of the *Tel Quel* group to involve a complex allegorical structure whose ultimate sense was script or language. In the same way, the various interpretations in terms of *exchange* (as in Jacques Ehrmann's analysis of Corneille's *Cinna*,[107] or Todorov's reading of the stories of the *Decameron*[108]) involve an implicit linguistic or communicational content to the degree to which Structuralism has consistently identified exchange and the linguistic circuit since Lévi-Strauss first assimilated Saussure's *Cours* to Marcel Mauss' *Essai sur le don* in his work on kinship systems. We find this auto-designation at work in yet another form in that implicit content which Greimas confers on the story-telling structure through his influential description of it as the breach and ultimate reestablishment of a contract.[109] Above and beyond the political implications of such a description, it is clear that, insofar as the notion of a social contract derives here from Lévi-Strauss, it means the origin of culture in general as law, or in short, as language itself. Such a projective effect or optical illusion may be observed in other, more peripheral types of research, such as that of Laplanche and Pontalis on Freud's concept of the phantasm, which, with its source in the primitive seduction scene and its privileged images of castration, they also ultimately interpret as a kind of reflection on origins, which is to say on its own origins as well.[110]

[107] Jacques Ehrmann, "Structures of Exchange in *Cinna*," in Michael Lane, ed., *Structuralism: A Reader* (London, 1970), pp. 222-247.

[108] In *Grammaire du Décaméron*, pp. 77-82.

[109] In *Sémantique structurale*, pp. 207-208.

[110] See Jean Laplanche and J.-B. Pontalis, "Fantasme originaire, fantasmes des origines, origine du fantasme," in *Temps modernes*, No. 215 (December, 1964), esp. pp. 1,854-1,855.

This is not to say that such interpretation is necessarily false. Just as the Formalists were right to claim, from their own perspective, that the essential content of every work is "nothing more" than the coming into being of that work itself, so also it is certain that there is a sense in which every enunciation involves a kind of lateral statement about language, which is to say about itself as well, and includes a kind of auto-designation within its very structure, signifies itself as an act of speech and as the reinvention of speech in general.

We owe the most complete explanation of this phenomenon to Roman Jakobson, who, thus completing the transfer of Formalist impulses to the new Structuralist problem-complex, now sees such auto-referentiality as the result of a particular and determinate imbalance in the communicational act as a whole. He sums up the structure of the latter as follows: "The ADDRESSER sends a MESSAGE to the ADDRESSEE. To be operative the message requires a CONTEXT referred to ('referent' in another, somewhat ambiguous, nomenclature), seizable by the addressee, and either verbal or capable of being verbalized; a CODE fully, or at least partially, common to the addresser and addressee (or in other words, to the encoder and decoder of the message); and, finally, a CONTACT, a physical channel and psychological connection between the addresser and the addressee, enabling both of them to enter and stay in communication. All these factors inalienably involved in verbal communication may be schematized as follows:

CONTEXT
MESSAGE
ADDRESSER . . . . ADDRESSEE
CONTACT
CODE

Each of these six factors determines a different function of language."[111] This is to say that the character of any linguistic utterance will depend essentially on which of these factors is emphasized at the expense of the others. Thus an emphasis on the addresser himself yields an "expressive" or "emotive" type of language, while one on the addressee may be thought of as a kind of vocative or imperative (the "conative" function). An orientation towards the context involves a referential or denotative emphasis, while that on the contact or channel of communication Jakobson characterizes, following Malinowski, as a "phatic" enunciation ("a profuse exchange of ritualized formulas . . . entire dialogues with the mere purport of prolonging communication. . .").[112] According to such an account, then, the "metalingual" function of language will be that which stresses the code used, a kind of "glossing" operation to which we have recourse "whenever the addresser and/or the addressee need to check up whether they use the same code"; while "the set (*Einstellung*) toward the MESSAGE as such, focus on the message for its own sake, is the POETIC function of language."[113]

Such a comprehensive and structural view of the linguistic act or object now permits us to see what we have called the auto-referentiality of narrative (e.g., the interpretation of a narrative in terms of language itself as some ultimate content) in historical and situational terms, rather than as some static and immutable property of all literature. For Jakobson, to be sure, the "Einstellung" toward the message factor is that which properly characterizes poetry as such; but this is perhaps more a directional signal than a historical claim. With respect to narrative analysis, however, it now becomes the task of any structural analysis

[111] Roman Jakobson, "Closing Statement: Linguistics and Poetics," in *Style in Language*, ed. Thomas A. Sebeok (Cambridge, Massachusetts, 1960), p. 353.
[112] *Ibid.*, p. 356.   [113] *Ibid.*, p. 357.

to understand the phenomenon of auto-referentiality in historical terms, or in other words to ground such interpretation in the logic of a determinate historical situation. When this is done, it will, I believe, transpire that such a geological shift of form into content is a relatively recent literary and linguistic phenomenon, but one which in modern times has become in some sense absolute. Thus, one can show how auto-referentiality dominates in some unconscious fashion even those contemporary works which lay claim to older and more traditional types of content: I think, for instance, of the novels of Simenon, which have been considered unmodern both in their referential aspects (Simenon's "psychology," his "knowledge of the human heart") and in the sturdiness of their plot structure, in appearance infinitely repeatable. The well-known formula places Maigret in the presence of a determinate character or psychological case study. Yet what is significant is that he ultimately solves the crime, not so much through rational deduction or inductive discovery, as through a leap of the imagination— Maigret's conclusions are based on the fact that he can or cannot visualize the character in question committing the crime which is to be solved. Maigret is thus called on to imagine, or indeed to reinvent, the character before him as a potentiality for a certain number of acts: what is this to say but that Maigret is before the suspect as the novelist is himself before his own characters? Maigret's "solution"— which permits yet another novel to be completed—is thus in reality merely a reduplication of that initial inspiration in which Simenon, visualizing his main character—criminal or suspect—conceived of the new book in the first place. This is to say something more and other than that Maigret is essentially Simenon himself: it is to claim that the very composition of the work is an unconscious self-portrait of the writer in the act of creating the work, a kind of peculiar structural deflection of that impulse which, on its way towards the real and towards some genuine referent, strikes a mirror instead without knowing it. We may thus say that the essential content of a Simenon novel is the act of writing novels, but that this content is itself concealed by the detective story form and disguised by the replacement of "writing" as such with the concepts of "imagination" and "psychological insight."

Insofar as it manifests itself in Structuralism itself, it is not hard to understand how such slippage from form to content is able to take place. The ambiguity lies in the notion of language itself, which designates both the abstract structure of speech, on the one hand, and the concrete social relationship of actual speaking, on the other. The imperceptible shift from one to the other of these meanings is perhaps most clearly apparent in Lacanian psychoanalysis, where one begins with the notion of a symbolic order (or in other words the pure and impersonal linguistic system itself), into which one then covertly reintroduces all the concrete content of the situation of the linguistic circuit, as a relationship of the I to the Other. The real content of such interpretation thus proves to derive, not from linguistic analysis, but from interpersonal relations. Nor does it do any good to object that the peculiar structure of language consists precisely in the built-in relationship to the other that it contains ("that semiotic law according to which the 'I' and the 'thou,' the emitter and receptor of an enunciation, always appear together"[114]): to say that all acts of speech are interpersonal relationships is not, as a proposition, the same as claiming that all interpersonal relationships are acts of speech.

[114] Todorov, *Littérature et signification*, p. 89.

7

"Well," I'd say, "I can't see anything." "Try it just once again," he'd say, and I would put my eye to the microscope and see nothing at all, except now and again a nebulous milky substance—a phenomenon of maladjustment. You were supposed to see a vivid, restless clockwork of sharply defined plant cells. "I see what looks like a lot of milk," I would tell him. This, he claimed, was the result of my not having adjusted the microscope properly, so he would readjust it for me, or rather, for himself. And I would look again and see milk.

—James Thurber, *My Life and Hard Times*

1. The imagery of the eye has often seemed to furnish a privileged language for the description of epistemological disorders. Thus Marx and Engels frequently described the illusions of idealism—the notion of the autonomy of culture and of the superstructure in general—as the result of an inversion which left facts upside down upon the retina of the eye.[115] I am tempted to have recourse to a related figure in order to account for the phenomena outlined above: the inability of a viewpoint for which history is but one possible type of discourse among others to deal historically with its material; and that even more symptomatic tendency of form to veer around into content, of a formalism to supply its structural absence of content by a hypostasis of its own method.

What happened to Thurber has always seemed to me emblematic, and not only of what happens to Structuralism. At length, he tells us, after much suffering and no less mistreatment at the hands of his exacerbated botany instructor, who "was beginning to quiver all over like Lionel Barrymore," he found himself suddenly able to see "a variegated constellation of flecks, specks, and dots." But the instructor is not as satisfied as the student with the drawing that re-

115 See my *Marxism and Form*, pp. 369-372.

sults. " 'That's your eye!' he shouted. 'You've fixed the lens so that it reflects! You've drawn your eye!' "[116]

I believe it is axiomatic that a philosophy which does not include within itself a theory of its own particular situation, which does not make a place for some essential self-consciousness along with the consciousness of the object with which it is concerned, which does not provide for some basic explanation of its own knowledge at the same time that it goes on knowing what it is supposed to know, is bound to end up drawing its own eye without realizing it. We need only think of Wittgenstein's game theory of language for an unrelated illustration: where after a while it becomes plain that what the philosopher is describing is not language in the absolute, but only the peculiar linguistic habits of philosophers of the Anglo-American school, who, working without books after the example of Socrates, turn their minds carefully inside out like old pockets in order to see what practical examples may be found there.

It will no doubt be objected that Structuralism does possess a theory of self-consciousness after all: it is precisely the concept of the metalanguage, which we have postponed discussing until this time. For the metalanguage is precisely the form that self-consciousness takes in the realm of language: it is language speaking of itself, a set of signs whose signified is itself a sign-system. It is thus the very vehicle for semiology's awareness of itself as a process, and as such reappears under various guises throughout Structuralism (in Althusser it takes the form of "theoretical practice," as opposed to mere ideology).

Yet I would more willingly describe it as the self-consciousness of a system which is structurally incapable of

[116] James Thurber, *The Thurber Carnival* (New York, 1945), p. 223.

evolving a theory of self-consciousness. It cannot perform the most basic function of genuine self-consciousness, which is to buckle the buckle, to reckon the place of the observer into the experiment, to put an end to the infinite regression which embarrasses Barthes in the following passage: "Human knowledge can participate in the becoming of the world only through a series of successive metalanguages, each one of which is alienated in the very moment that determines it. We may once again express this dialectic in formal terms: when he speaks of the rhetorical signified in his own metalanguage, the analyst inaugurates (or reassumes) an infinite type of knowledge-system: for should it happen for someone (someone else, or himself later on) to undertake an analysis of his writing and to attempt to reveal its latent content, it would be necessary for this someone to have recourse to a new metalanguage, which would in his turn expose him: and a day will inevitably come when structural analysis will pass to the rank of an object-language and be absorbed into a more complex system which will explain it in turn. This infinite construction is not sophisticated: it accounts for the transitory and somehow suspended objectivity of research, and confirms what we might call the Heracleitean characteristics of human knowledge, at any point *when by its object it is condemned to identify truth with language.* This is a necessity which Structuralism precisely attempts to understand, that is to say, to enunciate: the semiologist is he who expresses his future death in the very terms in which he has named and understood the world."[117] Thus synchronic certainty dissolves into the pathos of relativistic historicism: and this because a theory of models cannot recognize itself for a model without undoing the very premisses on which it is itself founded.

[117] Barthes, *Système de la mode*, p. 293, italics mine.

It is this peculiar regressive structure of the concept of metalanguage which accounts in particular for the stylistic characteristics of the Structuralists. They all, in one way or another, conceive of themselves as evolving commentaries on some more basic object language which is never given and which is ultimately at one with language itself: Barthes' adoption of the commentary form in S/Z, the systematic and as we have seen philosophically motivated reluctance of Derrida to use language as anything more than a gloss on the language of other philosophers (and indeed on their ideas about language)[118] are only the most extreme examples of an exegetic and second-degree structure common to all Structuralist thought. Hence their passion for mathematical formalizations, for graphs and visual schemata— so many Structuralist *hieroglyphs* designed to signify some ultimate object-language forever out of reach of the language of the commentary, and which is none other than Language itself. Hence also their styles: whether hermetic or white, whether the high style and classical pastiche of Lévi-Strauss or the bristling neologisms of Barthes, whether the self-conscious and over-elaborate preparatory coquetterie of Lacan or the grim and terroristic hectoring of Althusser—there is in all these styles a kind of distance from self, what one would like to call an unhappy consciousness on the stylistic level. By the terms of their own system they can never accede to the calm density of such a primary language as that of Hegel; and the professional duality of the Structuralists (who are both Structuralists and specialists in some one particular discipline) only reflects this initial stylistic and ontological dispersal.

2. The immediate result of such epistemological uncertainty is not theoretical but practical, for it is, I believe, re-

[118] Thus, Derrida's only direct presentation of his own "system" in "La Différance," *Tel Quel: Théorie d'ensemble,* takes the form of a kind of commentary on himself.

sponsible for the purely empirical framework which characterizes most of Structuralist research, a framework of which Michel Foucault has been the most explicit spokesman.[119] Under such conditions, the older specialized disciplines fail to dissolve into that vaster science of the concrete which Structuralism had seemed at other moments to project. Instead, they coexist in an uneasy rivalry which accounts for the exasperation of a Lévi-Strauss with philosophical criticisms of what he takes to be purely anthropological statements, or with that of a Greimas in the face of the extrapolation of the specialized operations of linguistics as a separate discipline into the apparently unrelated areas of psychoanalysis or politics.

In a more general way, we may note that it is precisely the close and carefully restricted work with a given text which prevents such issues from arising and being openly posed and resolved in their own terms. The very form of such research indefinitely postpones or indeed consigns to oblivion the theoretical antinomies which have been underscored in the present work; for they do not have to be dealt with during the analysis of an individual text and become problematical only in considering the relationship of one text to another, or indeed of one form of analysis to another. This is the basic thrust and motivation of empiricism in general, whether of the classical British school, or of Nietzsche (following Gilles Deleuze's interpretation of him as an essentially anti-Hegelian, anti-dialectical thinker), or of modern logical positivism: to substitute the discrete, the particular, for the concrete in the dialectical sense, to isolate the individual datum in such a way that its relationship to the totality never has to be dealt with because the latter never comes into view. The practical advantage of such an

[119] See in particular his *Archéologie du savoir* (Paris, 1969).

approach is that it permits work in a given field while adjourning the more vexing and somehow metaphysical problems of its basic philosophical presuppositions. Its ideological effect is, however, to prevent the ultimate return of the specialized intellectual discipline to that concrete social and historical situation in which it is of necessity grounded. Thus a school of thought whose dialectical mechanisms seemed initially to distinguish it from the empiricist procedures of such thinkers as Ogden and Richards proves in the long run in its practice to merit analogous philosophical objection.

3. The same ontological dispersal, the same discrete and empirical fragmentation, makes itself felt when we attempt to determine the status of the referent, the existence of which the theory of signs affirms at the same time that it brackets it. The problem is a particularly crucial one when we raise the kinds of questions with which Marxism has to deal, such as the relationship of superstructure to infrastructure. Do we then have to deal with the problem of the place of language itself in social life, a problem hotly debated in the Soviet Union during the Marr controversy, and liquidated, rather than resolved, by Stalin ("Briefly, language cannot be ranked either among bases or among superstructures")?[120] But in the present context we must repudiate the problem as such, insofar as it amounts to a hypostasis of Language: for there exist only specific languages and language systems, or better still, specific linguistic objects and acts, signs of various types already existing empirically in the world around us and entertaining the most varied kinds of relationships with the other components of the historical totality. Yet is not such a refusal of the very concept of Language (or of Meaning) tanta-

[120] Joseph Stalin, *Marxism and Linguistics* (New York, 1951), pp. 33-34.

mount to a repudiation of the very starting point and fundamental presupposition of Structuralist research itself?

To say, as the most consequent theoreticians of Structuralism have, that there can be no problem of the referent, inasmuch as the latter finds itself constantly reabsorbed into language in the form of new sign-systems, is merely to displace the problem, which remains intact. For one would be only too willing to admit that the infrastructure is itself a sign-system, or a complex of such systems, in its own right: what remains to be determined, however, is the precise nature of the relationship of such systems to those more overtly verbal ones which Marxism sees as forming the superstructure. Both synchrony and diachrony are involved: for it is not only a question of the coordination of two or more systems "at the same time," but also of the coordination between the changes taking place in each both separately and simultaneously.

Structuralism seems to have evolved two rather different strategies in its attempt to resolve this problem, which is not merely a theoretical one but bears very directly on the form and direction taken by practical research. The first solution, and the more satisfactory of the two, reminds me of Sartre's concept of the infrastructure or of socially conditioning factors as a *situation* to which events of the cultural dimension are a kind of reaction or response. Such is Lévi-Strauss' conception of myth or of primitive art as an imaginary resolution of some real social contradiction; and as I have indicated elsewhere, for all practical purposes such a description seems to me perfectly consistent with Marxism, in that it undertakes to reveal the function of ideological objects in the conjunctures of class struggle or economic development.[121] Althusser's solution, for which thought and theory readjust according to shifts and restructurations on

[121] See my *Marxism and Form*, pp. 375-384.

the more fundamental level of the problematic itself, would seem to be consistent with this view of Lévi-Strauss: it has, however, the merit of showing that an acceptable working solution is nonetheless not theoretically completely satisfactory, for its very terms replace us squarely before the unsolved problem of the relationship between changes in the problematic and those in the "real world." That this problem is not really solved by Lévi-Strauss either will be understood when we recall that what Lévi-Strauss calls a *contradiction* ought more properly to be termed an *antinomy*, a dilemma for the human mind, and it is the latter which somehow "reflects" some more basic contradiction in social life. The theoretical question of the nature of such "reflexion" or relationship thus remains open, whatever results the analytical practice may have had.

By far the most common strategy to which the Structuralists have had recourse in dealing with this question is however the concept of the *homology* or the *isomorphism*. The first of these terms was popularized by Lucien Goldmann, whose work, if not properly Structuralist in the present sense, nonetheless suggested this strategic technique for demonstrating structural parallelisms between the various "levels" of a phenomenon, e.g., between a tragedy of Racine and the ideology of Port-Royal, between the form of the nineteenth century novel and the structure of the market system itself. Such a static view of the interrelationship of structural levels does not seem to me essentially different—in spite of its greater methodological and analytical rigor—from the kind of total period style evoked in the works of Taine and Spengler; and no doubt every beginning exploration of a given period attempts to discover in some such way the specificity of its thought structures, and to come to some precise awareness of the unique relationship between those thought structures and the other, equally specific structures obtaining in the social and economic realities of the period.

But surely nothing is accomplished by the abstract assurance that the structures of these various levels are "the same." In practice, indeed, it turns out that it is much easier to extract linguistic structures from cultural objects which are already of a linguistic character, than from the economic realm itself: such homologies often prove to be little more than hasty projections of the former upon the latter, so that the subsequent "identity" between the two thus does not really come as much of a surprise. Even where this is not the case, there remains the danger that the identity holds good, not for the concrete realities themselves, but merely for the conceptual abstractions that have been derived from them. Insofar as such a doctrine encourages intellectuals in the belief that with a little ingenuity their analysis of historical reality can be manufactured inside their own heads, it reinforces their occupational idealism by isolating consciousness from the resistance of the infrastructural context and the social ground itself; as a method, therefore, the search for homologies is open to ideological, as well as theoretical, criticism.

4. From the point of view of epistemological theory it has been suggested that it is rather to the dilemmas of Kantian critical philosophy that, consciously or unconsciously, Structuralism remains a prisoner.[122] At the conclusion of our examination, such an unconscious recapitulation of the philosophical tradition does not seem altogether without its advantages. For we know, in a sense, the sequel to the story, and are well aware how a kind of historicizing and dialectical thought was able to convert the static Kanti-

[122] "A Kantianism without a transcendental subject," as Ricoeur has described it (Paul Ricoeur, *Le Conflit des interprétations* [Paris, 1969], p. 55).

an description of the mental categories into historical moments in an unfolding logic or process; how in this new perspective the hitherto unknowable *Ding-an-sich* suddenly proved to be no more than a single determinate articulation in that complex of relationships between subject and object which makes up experience itself. This is how Lukács describes the transformation of the older static logical categories by the Hegelian dialectic: "To have understood that the signifying capacity of the most abstract categories provides a means for presenting the latter in their movement and their interrelationship; that in this sense the 'lack of content' of formal logic merely stands as an extreme case of the latter's signifying capacity itself; that for that very reason the various problems of objective reality and of man's subjective cognition constitute the object of [some new] dialectical logic . . . such an achievement was Hegel's alone."[123] One cannot, of course, think such a philosophical reconversion otherwise than as a prodigious dialectical shifting of gears, and the mere recommendation is, taken by itself, a purely formal one, empty of any real content.

Hence the interest for us of Greimas' recent reflections on the tasks which confront that discipline which he has come to think of as a semiotics rather than a semantics or a semiology. Such a discipline, insofar as it takes the very production of meaning as its object, finds itself obliged to come to terms with that infinite regress from signifier to signified, from linguistic object to metalanguage, which we have frequently had occasion to underscore in the preceding pages. It does so now, however, by including such an infinite regress in its very vision of the nature of meaning: "Signification is thus nothing but such transposition from one level of language to another, from one language to a dif-

---

[123] Georg Lukács, *Der Junge Hegel* (Berlin, 1954), p. 508.

ferent language, and meaning is nothing but the possibility of such *transcoding*."[124]

Truth as transcoding, as translation from one code to another—I would myself have preferred to say (following an analogous expression of Greimas himself) that the truth-effect involves or results from just such a conceptual operation. This would be a perfectly exact formal definition of the process of arriving at truth, even though it would presuppose nothing about the content of that truth, nor would it necessarily imply that every such transcoding operation results in a truth-effect of equal strength or "validity." Yet such a formula would have the advantage—in Derrida's sense—of freeing structural analysis from the myth of structure itself, of some permanent and spatial-like organization of the object. It would place the "object" between parentheses, and consider the analytic practice as "nothing but" an operation in time. It would thus for the first time permit the description of the Structuralist procedure as a genuine *hermeneutics*—although one which would have little to do with the theological overtones which that term has acquired, with Ricoeur, in France, and with Gadamer, in Germany. Indeed, the hermeneutic here foreseen would, by disclosing the presence of preexisting codes and models and by reemphasizing the place of the analyst himself, reopen text and analytic process alike to all the winds of history. There is no immutable fatality at work in the history of philosophy to bring such a new methodological development to pass. Yet it is only, it seems to me, at the price of such a development, or of something like it, that the twin, apparently incommensurable, demands of synchronic analysis and historical awareness, of structure and self-consciousness, language and history, can be reconciled.

[124] A. J. Greimas, *Du Sens*, p. 13.

Bibliography

Althusser, Louis. *Lénine et la philosophie*. Paris: Maspéro, 1969.

Lire le Capital. 2 vols. Paris: Maspéro, 1968.

Montesquieu. Paris: Presses universitaires de France, 1959.

Pour Marx. Paris: Maspéro, 1965.

Alonso, Amado. "Prólogo a la edición española," in F. de Saussure, *Curso de lingüística general* (Buenos Aires: Editorial Losada, 1945), pp. 7-30.

Alonso, Damaso. *Poesía española: Ensayo de Métodos y Límites Estilísticos*. Madrid: Editorial Gredos, 1962.

Ambrogio, Ignazio. *Formalismo e avanguardia in Russia*. Rome: Editori Reuniti, 1968.

Barthes, Roland. *Critique et vérité*. Paris: Seuil, 1964.

L'Empire des signes. Geneva: Skira, 1970.

Essais critiques. Paris: Seuil, 1964.

Michelet par lui-même. Paris: Seuil, 1965.

Mythologies. Paris: Seuil, 1957.

Sade, Fourier, Loyola. Paris: Seuil, 1971.

Sur Racine. Paris: Seuil, 1963.

Système de la mode. Paris: Seuil, 1967.

S/Z. Paris: Seuil, 1971.

Benveniste, Émile. *Problèmes de linguistique générale*. Paris: Gallimard, 1966.

Blanché, Robert. *Les Structures intellectuelles*. Paris: Vrin, 1966.

Brecht, Bertolt. *Schriften zum Theater*. Frankfurt: Suhrkamp, 1957.

217

BIBLIOGRAPHY

Bremond, Claude. "La Logique des possibles narratifs." *Communications*, No. 8 (Spring, 1966), pp. 60-76.

"Le Message narratif." *Communications*, No. 4 (Winter, 1964), pp. 4-32.

Brøndall, Vigo. *Essais de linguistique générale*. Copenhagen: Einar Munksgaard, 1943.

Théorie des prépositions. Copenhagen: Einar Munksgaard, 1950.

Bukharin, Nikolai. "O formalnom metode v isskustve." *Krasnaya Nov*, Vol. III (1925), pp. 248-257.

Chomsky, Noam. *Current Issues in Linguistic Theory*. The Hague: Mouton, 1964.

De Mallac, Guy, and Eberbach, Margaret. *Roland Barthes*. Paris: Editions universitaires, 1971.

De Man, Paul. "Rhetorique de la cécité." *Poétique*, No. 4 (Winter, 1970), pp. 455-475.

Derrida, Jacques. *De la grammatologie*. Paris: Editions de minuit, 1967.

L'Écriture et la différence. Paris: Seuil, 1967.

"La Pharmacie de Platon." *Tel Quel*, No. 32 (Winter, 1968), pp. 3-48; and No. 33 (Spring, 1968), pp. 18-59.

La Voix et le phénomène. Paris: Presses universitaires de France, 1967.

Doroszewski, W. "Quelques remarques sur les rapports de la sociologie et de la linguistique: Durkheim et F. de Saussure." *Journal de psychologie normale et pathologique*, Vol. XXX (1933), pp. 82-91.

Dundes, Alan. *The Morphology of North American Indian Folktales*. FF Communications No. 195. Helsinki: Suomalainen Tiedeakatemia, 1964.

Eco, Umberto. *La Struttura assente*. Milan: Bompiani, 1968.

Ehrmann, Jacques, ed. *Structuralism*. Yale French Studies, Nos. 36-37 (October, 1966).

218

BIBLIOGRAPHY

Eichenbaum, Boris. *Aufsätze zur Theorie und Geschichte der Literatur.* Edited and translated by A. Kaempfe. Frankfurt: Suhrkamp, 1965.

Lermontov. Leningrad, 1924.

Literatura (Teoria, Kritika, Polemika). Leningrad, 1927.

O. Henry and the Theory of the Short Story. Translated by I. R. Titunik. Ann Arbor: Michigan Slavic Contributions, 1968.

Eisenstein, Sergei. *Film Form and the Film Sense.* New York: Meridian, 1957.

Erlich, Victor. *Russian Formalism.* The Hague: Mouton, 1955.

Faye, Jean-Pierre, and Robel, Léon, eds. "Le Cercle de Prague." *Change,* No. 3 (Fall, 1969).

Foucault, Michel. *Archéologie du savoir.* Paris: Gallimard, 1969.

Histoire de la folie. Paris: Plon, 1961.

Les Mots et les choses. Paris: Gallimard, 1966.

Garvin, Paul, ed. and trans. *A Prague School Reader on Esthetics, Literary Structure, and Style.* Washington, D.C.: Washington Linguistics Club, 1955.

Geyl, Pieter. *Debates with Historians.* London: Batsford, 1955.

Godel, Robert. *Les Sources manuscrites du Cours de linguistique générale de F. De Saussure.* Geneva: Droz, 1957.

Greimas, A. J. *Du Sens.* Paris: Seuil, 1970.

Sémantique structurale. Paris: Larousse, 1966.

Guillén, Claudio. *Literature as System.* Princeton: Princeton University Press, 1971.

Hayes, E. Nelson, and Hayes, Tanya, editors. *Claude Lévi-Strauss: The Anthropologist as Hero.* Cambridge, Massachusetts: MIT Press, 1970.

BIBLIOGRAPHY

Hjelmslev, Louis. *Prolegomena to a Theory of Language.* Trans. by F. J. Whitfield. Madison: University of Wisconsin Press, 1963.

Ivić, Milka. *Trends in Linguistics.* The Hague: Mouton, 1965.

Jakobson, Roman. "Closing Statement: Linguistics and Poetics," in *Style in Language,* ed. Thomas A. Sebeok (Cambridge, Mass.: MIT Press, 1960), pp. 350-377.

Essais de linguistique générale. Paris: Editions de minuit, 1963.

"Principes de phonologie historique," in Troubetskoy, N. S., *Principes de phonologie* (Paris, 1964), pp. 315-336.

"Une Microscopie du dernier *Spleen* dans les *Fleurs du mal.*" *Tel Quel,* No. 29 (Spring, 1967), pp. 12-24.

"Randbemerkungen zur Prosa des Dichters Pasternak." *Slavische Rundschau,* Vol. vii (1935), pp. 357-374.

"Two Aspects of Language and Two Types of Aphasic Disturbances." In R. Jakobson and M. Halle, *Fundamentals of Language* (The Hague: Mouton, 1956), pp. 55-82.

(with P. Bogatyrev:) "Die Folklore als eine besondere Form des Schaffens." *Selected Writings,* Vol. iv (The Hague: Mouton, 1966), pp. 1-15.

(with C. Lévi-Strauss:) "*Les Chats.*" *L'Homme,* Vol. ii, No. 1 (January-April, 1962), pp. 5-21.

Köngäs, Elli-Kaija, and Miranda, Pierre. "Structural Models in Folklore." *Midwest Folklore,* Vol. xii, No. 3 (Fall, 1962), pp. 133-192.

Kristeva, Julia. *Semeiōtikē: Recherches pour une sémanalyse.* Paris: Seuil, 1969.

Kuhn, T. S. *The Structure of Scientific Revolutions.* Chicago: University of Chicago Press, 1962.

Lacan, Jacques. *Écrits.* Paris: Seuil, 1966.

Lane, Michael, ed. *Structuralism: a Reader.* London: Jonathan Cape, 1970.

Lemon, Lee T. and Reis, Marian J., eds. and trans. *Russian Formalist Criticism: Four Essays.* Lincoln: University of Nebraska Press, 1965.

Leroy, Maurice. *Les Grands courants de la linguistique moderne.* Brussels: Presses universitaires de Bruxelles, 1966.

Lévi-Strauss, Claude. *Anthropologie structurale.* Paris: Plon, 1958.

Le Cru et le cuit. Paris: Plon, 1964.

Du miel aux cendres. Paris: Plon, 1966.

"La Geste d'Asdiwal." *Temps modernes,* No. 179 (March, 1961), pp. 1,080-1,123.

L'Origine des manières de table. Paris: Plon, 1968.

La Pensée sauvage. Paris: Plon, 1962.

The Scope of Anthropology. London: Jonathan Cape, 1967.

"La Structure et la Forme." *Cahiers de l'institut de science économique appliquée,* No. 99 (March, 1960), pp. 3-36.

Les Structures élémentaires de la parenté. Paris: Presses universitaires de France, 1949.

Le Totémisme aujourd'hui. Paris: Presses universitaires de France, 1962.

Tristes tropiques. Paris: Plon, 1955.

Lotman, Iurii M. *Lektsii po Struktural'noi Poetike.* Providence, R.I.: Brown University Press, 1968.

Struktura khudozhestvennogo teksta. Providence, R.I.: Brown University Press, 1971.

Marin, Louis. *Sémiotique de la Passion.* Paris: Bibiliothèque de Sciences Religieuses, 1971.

221

BIBLIOGRAPHY

Matejka, Ladislav, and Pomorska, Krystyna, editors. *Readings in Russian Poetics: Formalist and Structuralist Views*. Cambridge, Massachusetts: M.I.T. Press, 1971.

Merleau-Ponty, Maurice. *Signes*. Paris: Gallimard, 1960.

Ogden, C. K., and Richards, I. A. *The Meaning of Meaning*. London: Routledge and Kegan Paul, 1960.

Ong, Walter J. *The Presence of the Word*. New Haven: Yale University Press, 1967.

Oulanoff, Hongor. *The Serapion Brothers*. The Hague: Mouton, 1966.

Pomorska, Krystyna. *Russian Formalist Theory and its Poetic Ambiance*. The Hague: Mouton, 1968.

Problèmes du structuralisme. Les Temps modernes, No. 246 (November, 1966).

Propp, Vladimir. *The Morphology of the Folk Tale*. Trans. by Lawrence Scott. Austin: University of Texas Press, 1968.

Qu'est-ce que le structuralisme? Paris: Seuil, 1968.

Ricoeur, Paul. *Le Conflit des interprétations*. Paris: Seuil, 1969.

Rifflet-Lemaire, Anika. *Jacques Lacan*. Brussels: Charles Dessart, 1970.

Saussure, Ferdinand de. *Cours de linguistique générale*. Paris: Presses universitaires de France, 1965.
Edition critique du Cours. Edited by Rudolf Engler. 3 vols. Wiesbaden: Harrassowitz, 1967.

Scholes, Robert. *Structuralism in Literature*. New Haven: Yale University Press, 1974.

Sebag, Lucien, *Marxisme et structuralisme*. Paris: Payot, 1964.

Sheldon, Richard. *Viktor Borisovič Shklovsky: Literary Theory and Practice 1914-1930*. Ann Arbor: University Microfilms, 1966.

Shklovsky, Viktor. *Erinnerungen an Majakovskij*. Trans. by R. Reimar. Frankfurt: Insel, 1966.

O teorii prozy. Moscow, 1929.

Schriften zum Film. Trans. by A. Kaempfe. Frankfurt: Suhrkamp, 1966.

A Sentimental Journey. Trans. by Richard Sheldon. Ithaca: Cornell University Press, 1970.

Theorie der Prosa. Trans. by Gisela Drohla. Frankfurt: Fischer, 1966.

Sollers, Philippe. *Logiques*, Paris: Seuil, 1968.

Stalin, Joseph. *Marxism and Linguistics*. New York: International, 1951.

Tel Quel: Théorie d'ensemble. Paris: Seuil, 1968.

Todorov, Tzvetan. *Grammaire du Décaméron*. The Hague: Mouton, 1969.

Introduction à la littérature fantastique. Paris: Seuil, 1969.

Littérature et signification. Paris: Larousse, 1967.

Poétique de la prose. Paris: Seuil, 1971.

(editor and translator:) *Théorie de la littérature*. Paris; Seuil, 1965.

Tomashevsky, Boris. "La Nouvelle école d'histoire littéraire en Russie." *Revue des études slaves*, Vol. viii (1928), pp. 226-240.

Trier, Jost. *Der deutsche Wortschatz im Sinnbezirk des Verstandes*. Heidelberg: Winter, 1931.

Trotsky, Leon. *Literature and Revolution*. New York: Russell and Russell, 1957.

Troubetskoy, N. S. *Principes de phonologie*. Paris: Klincksieck, 1964.

Tynyanov, Yury. *Arkhaisty i novatory*. Leningrad, 1929.

Die literarischen Kunstmittel und die Evolution in der Literatur. Ed. and trans. by A. Kaempfe. Frankfurt: Suhrkamp, 1967.

Problema stikhvortnogo yazyka. Leningrad, 1924.

BIBLIOGRAPHY

Uitti, Karl D. *Linguistics and Literary Theory*. Englewood Cliffs, N.J.: Prentice-Hall, 1969.

Wilden, A. G. *The Language of the Self*. Baltimore: Johns Hopkins Press, 1968.

Index

225

PRINCETON ESSAYS IN LITERATURE

Advisory Committee
Robert Fagles, A. Bartlett Giamatti, Claudio Guillén,
Theodore Ziolkowski

The Orbit of Thomas Mann
By Erich Kahler

On Four Modern Humanists:
Hofmannsthal, Gundolf, Curtius, Kantorowicz
Edited by Arthur R. Evans, Jr.

Flaubert and Joyce: The Rite of Fiction
By Richard Cross

A Stage for Poets: Studies in the
Theatre of Hugo and Musset
By Charles Affron

Hofmannsthal's Novel "Andreas"
By David Miles

On Gide's Prométhée: Private Myth and
Public Mystification
By Kurt Weinberg

Kazantzakis and the Linguistic Revolution
in Greek Literature
By Peter Bien

Modern Greek Writers
Edited by Edmund Keeley and Peter Bien

Wallace Stevens and the Symbolist Imagination
By Michel Benamou

The Inner Theatre of
Recent French Poetry
By Mary Ann Caws

Cervantes' Christian Romance:
a Study of Persiles y Sigismunda
By Alban K. Forcione

The Prison-House of Language:
A Critical Account of
Structuralism and Russian
Formalism
By Fredric Jameson